Second Edition

Strategic Reading 3

D1268195

Jack C. Richards   Samuela Eckstut-Didier

CAMBRIDGE
UNIVERSITY PRESS

32 Avenue of the Americas, New York, NY 10013-2473, USA

Cambridge University Press is part of the University of Cambridge.

It furthers the University's mission by disseminating knowledge in the pursuit of education, learning and research at the highest international levels of excellence.

www.cambridge.org
Information on this title: www.cambridge.org/9780521281119

First published 2012
3rd printing 2014

Printed in Hong Kong, China, by Golden Cup Printing Company Limited

A catalog record for this publication is available from the British Library.

ISBN 978-0-521-28111-9 Student's Book
ISBN 978-0-521-28116-4 Teacher's Manual

Book design: TSI Graphics
Layout services: Page Designs International, Inc.
Photo research: TSI Graphics

Contents

Scope and Sequence

Unit	Readings	Reading Strategies
Unit 1 **Superstitions**	**1** Two Worlds **2** Lucky Hats and Other Fishing Superstitions **3** A Superstition About New Calendars	Making Inferences Predicting Previewing Vocabulary Scanning Skimming Summarizing Thinking About the Topic Understanding Pronoun Reference
Unit 2 **Health**	**1** Diets of the World **2** Drink, Blink, and Rest **3** Azeri Hills Hold Secret of Long Life	Identifying Main Ideas and Supporting Details Predicting Recognizing Cause and Effect Skimming Thinking About the Topic Thinking About What You Know Understanding Pronoun Reference
Unit 3 **Remarkable Talents**	**1** The Memory Man **2** Born to Paint: Alexandra Nechita **3** Hyper-polyglots	Making Inferences Predicting Reading Critically Recognizing Point of View Skimming Thinking About What You Know
Unit 4 **Beauty**	**1** Executives Go Under the Knife **2** What Makes a Man Attractive? **3** In the Land of the Mirror	Predicting Skimming Summarizing Thinking About the Topic Understanding Pronoun Reference Understanding Text Organization
Unit 5 **Technology**	**1** Affectionate Androids **2** Identification, Please! **3** Researchers Worry as Cyber-teens Grow Up	Identifying Main Ideas and Supporting Details Making Inferences Predicting Previewing Vocabulary Recognizing Purpose Scanning Skimming Thinking About the Topic
Unit 6 **Punishment**	**1** Spanking on Trial **2** The Letter **3** Schools Take the Fun Out of Suspension	Making Inferences Predicting Previewing Vocabulary Recognizing Point of View Recognizing Purpose Scanning Skimming Thinking About the Topic

Introduction

Overview

Strategic Reading is a three-level series for young adult and adult learners of English. As its title suggests, the series is designed to develop strategies for reading, vocabulary-building, and critical thinking. Each level features texts from a variety of authentic sources, including newspapers, magazines, books, and Web sites. The series encourages students to examine important topics in their lives as they build essential reading skills.

The third level in the series, *Strategic Reading 3*, is aimed at low-advanced level students. It contains 12 units divided into three readings on popular themes such as superstition, talent, technology, and fashion. The readings in *Strategic Reading 3* range in length from 450 to 600 words, and they are accompanied by a full range of activities.

The units (and the readings within units) can either be taught in the order they appear or out of sequence. The readings and exercises, however, increase in difficulty as students progress through the book.

The Unit Structure

Each unit has the same 10-page structure. It includes a one-page unit preview and three readings, each of which is accompanied by two pre-reading tasks and four post-reading tasks.

Unit Preview
Each unit begins with a brief summary of the three readings in the unit. These summaries are followed by questions that stimulate students' interest in the readings and allow them to share their knowledge of the topic.

Pre-reading Tasks
Each reading is accompanied by two pre-reading tasks: a reading preview task and a skimming or scanning task.

Reading Preview
Before each reading, students complete one of four types of pre-reading exercises: *Predicting*, *Previewing vocabulary*, *Thinking about the topic*, or *Thinking about what you know*. These exercises prepare students to read and help them connect the topic of the reading to their own lives. Students identify information they expect to read, learn new vocabulary, and write down what they know about the topic or mark statements that are true about themselves.

Skimming/Scanning

One *Skimming* or *Scanning* exercise accompanies every reading. Before reading the whole text, students learn either to scan a text to look for specific information or to skim a text to get the gist. Other activities in this section ask students to confirm predictions from the reading preview section, compare their experiences with the writer's experiences, or identify the writer's opinion.

Post-Reading Tasks

There are four post-reading tasks (A–D) following each reading. These tasks respectively check students' comprehension, build their vocabulary, help them develop a reading strategy, and provide an opportunity for discussion.

A Comprehension Check

The task immediately following the reading is designed to check students' comprehension. In some cases, students check their understanding of the main ideas. In others, students have to delve more deeply into the text for more detailed information.

B Vocabulary Study

This section is designed to help students understand six to eight words that appear in the text. Students use contextual clues, recognize similarity in meaning between words, or categorize words according to meaning.

C Reading Strategy

An important part of *Strategic Reading* is reading strategy development. Students are introduced to a variety of strategies, such as making inferences, summarizing, and understanding pronoun reference. (For a full list of reading strategies, see the Scope and Sequence on pages iv–v.) Practicing these strategies will help students gain a deeper understanding of the content of the text and develop the necessary strategies they will need to employ when they read on their own outside of the classroom. The section opens with a brief explanation of the reading strategy and why it is important.

D Relating Reading to Personal Experience

This section asks three open-ended questions that are closely connected to the topic of the reading. It gives students an opportunity to share their thoughts, opinions, and experiences in discussion or in writing. It is also a chance to review and use vocabulary introduced in the text.

Timed Reading

Each unit ends with an invitation for students to complete a timed reading task. Students are instructed to re-read one of the texts in the unit, presumably the one they understand best, and to time themselves as they read. They then record their time in the chart on page 124 so that they can check their progress as they proceed through the book. (Naturally, there is no harm in students re-reading and timing themselves on every text in a unit. However, this could be de-motivating for all but the most ambitious of students.)

Reading Strategies

Reading is a process that involves interaction between a reader and a text. A successful reader is a strategic reader who adjusts his or her approach to a text by considering questions such as the following:

- What is my purpose in reading this text? Am I reading it for pleasure? Am I reading it to keep up-to-date on current events? Will I need this information later (for a test, for example)?
- What kind of text is this? Is it an advertisement, a poem, a news article, or some other kind of text?
- What is the writer's purpose? Is it to persuade, to entertain, or to inform the reader?
- What kind of information do I expect to find in the text?
- What do I already know about texts of this kind? How are they usually organized?
- How should I read this text? Should I read it to find specific information, or should I look for the main ideas? Should I read it again carefully to focus on the details?
- What linguistic difficulties does the text pose? How can I deal with unfamiliar vocabulary, complex sentences, and lengthy sentences and paragraphs?
- What is my opinion about the content of the text?

Reading strategies are the decisions readers make in response to questions like these. They may prompt the reader to make predictions about the content and organization of a text based on background knowledge of the topic as well as familiarity with the text type. They may help the reader decide the rate at which to read the text – a quick skim for main ideas; a scan for specific information; a slower, closer reading for more detailed comprehension; or a rapid reading to build fluency. Other reading strategies help the reader make sense of the relationships among the ideas, such as cause and effect, contrast, and so on. In addition, the strategy of reading a text critically – reacting to it and formulating opinions about the content – is a crucial part of being a successful reader.

The *Strategic Reading* series develops fluency and confidence in reading by developing the student's repertoire of reading strategies. Students learn how to approach a text, how to choose appropriate strategies for reading a text, how to think critically about what they read, and how to deal with the difficulties that different kinds of texts may pose.

Jack C. Richards

Authors' Acknowledgments

We would like to thank Bernard Seal for his efforts in getting the project going, for his vision in setting the second edition down a new path, and for his insightful comments until the very end.

We are also grateful to the production and design staff that worked on this new edition of *Strategic Reading*: our in-house editors, Alan Kaplan and Brigit Dermott; TSI Graphics; and Don Williams, who did the composition.

For their useful comments and suggestions, many thanks to the reviewers: Laurie Blackburn, Cleveland High School, Seattle, Washington; Alain Gallie, Interactive College of Technology, Atlanta, Georgia; John Howrey, Nanzan University, Nagoya, Japan; Ana Morales de Leon, Instituto Tecnologico de Monterrey, Monterrey, Mexico; Sheryl Meyer, American Language Institute, University of Denver, Denver, Colorado; Donna Murphy-Tovalin, Lone Star College, Houston, Texas; Richard Patterson, King Saud University, Saudi Arabia; Byongchul Seo, Yonsei University, Seoul, South Korea.

Finally, a writer is nobody without a good editor. In that vein, we are grateful to Amy Cooper and Kathleen O'Reilly for their critical eye and their expert guidance. And to Amy Cooper in her role as project manager, we owe many thanks for her patience, understanding, and good sense of humor.

Jack C. Richards
Sydney, Australia

Sammi Eckstut
Melrose, Massachusetts, USA

UNIT 1 Superstitions

Look at the titles of the readings and their brief descriptions to preview this unit's content. Before you begin each reading, answer the questions about it.

Reading 1 | **Two Worlds**

In this excerpt from her memoir, the writer talks about her childhood fascination with tales of superstition.

1. Who used to tell you stories when you were a child? Did you believe that all the stories were true? Explain your answer.

2. In some cultures, people think it's bad luck to walk under a ladder. What are some examples of superstitions in your culture?

3. Can a person who believes in superstitions also be a rational person who can make decisions based on thought and not just feelings? Why or why not?

Reading 2 | **Lucky Hats and Other Fishing Superstitions**

What are some common superstitions among fishermen? You can find out in this newspaper article.

1. Would you like to go fishing? Why or why not?

2. What equipment do you need to go fishing?

3. Do you think you need luck to have success when you go fishing? Why or why not?

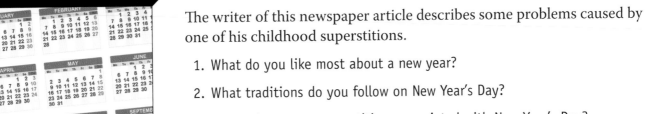

Reading 3 | **A Superstition About New Calendars**

The writer of this newspaper article describes some problems caused by one of his childhood superstitions.

1. What do you like most about a new year?

2. What traditions do you follow on New Year's Day?

3. Do you know any superstitions associated with New Year's Day?

Two Worlds

Previewing Vocabulary

The words in the box are from the reading. Discuss the meanings of the words with a partner. Look up any new words in a dictionary.

curses	miracles	roots and herbs
saints	souls of the dead	the evil eye

Scanning

Scan the reading. Find and circle the words from the box. Then discuss how you think these words relate to the topic of the reading.

This excerpt from her autobiography is about Gabriella de Ferrari's childhood in Peru.

1   Early in life, I realized that there were two very different ways of looking at the world, my parents' and Señorita Luisa's. What she told me was what I assumed the world outside my house believed. At home what I was told was what people believed in that faraway place where my parents came from. I kept them separate and functioned accordingly, never suffering from the difference, at least while I was young and the lines were so easy to draw. Yet Señorita Luisa's world, together with that of the maids in the kitchen, was far more seductive than the rational world of my parents. I liked curses and miracles, and praying for a handsome husband, and buying up heaven.

Mother and Señorita Luisa talked to each other constantly. They would sit under a large mulberry tree in the afternoon and become absorbed in each other's stories. My own time with Señorita Luisa came in the evenings, when I got back from school. I would go to her house for a snack of hot chocolate and a cake she made especially for me of fresh figs held together with what she called "honey glue." She had many stories to tell, and they were all equally outrageous. I listened, mesmerized by her tales delivered in the monotonous rhythms of her voice as if they occurred every day, like drinking milk or taking a bath.

One of my favorite activities, in which Señorita Luisa would indulge me only when she was in a good mood, was to have my fortune read. She would drip hot wax from a candle into a large container of icy water. When the wax hit the water, it formed different shapes. She read them and told me my "little future," that is, my future for the next week. The prognostications[1] were mostly designed to teach me to behave: "This week you will tell a lie and that will cost you, because your mother will not believe you anymore." Only occasionally would she tell me my "big future," the one I wanted to hear the most: A handsome man would fall in love with me, a man with green eyes and dark hair like Luisa's brothers.

The maids in my family's kitchen were also constantly reading wax, but they weren't allowed to read wax for me. My mother thought it was nonsense. She never knew that Señorita Luisa read my fortune. Señorita Luisa also told ghost stories about the *almas*, the souls of the dead that came to visit at night. She used to scare me so much I had to ask Saturnina to stay with me until I fell asleep. Saturnina knew how to send the souls away: She tied a black ribbon to the window and left them a piece of bread.

As Señorita Luisa had saints, Saturnina and the other maids had roots and herbs. These could perform any kind of miracle, especially scaring away the "evil eye" that women gave each other when they were interested in the same man. I was constantly torn between wanting to believe Señorita Luisa and Saturnina and wanting to believe Mother, who was more interested in having me worry about geography and math.

---

[1] *prognostications:* predictions

Adapted from *Gringa Latina*

A Comprehension Check

Check (✓) the statement that best expresses the main idea of the reading.

_____ 1. The writer's mother paid Señorita Luisa to teach her daughter about superstitions, something that every young girl should learn.

_____ 2. As a child, the writer loved being with the maids and Señorita Luisa more than she liked being with her parents.

_____ 3. As a child, the writer lived in a world where many people believed in superstitions, but her parents didn't.

B Vocabulary Study

Find the words in *italics* in the reading. Then circle the correct meaning of each word.

1. When something is *seductive*, it is **attractive** / **frightening** / **painful**. (par. 1)

2. When something is *outrageous*, it **is very unusual and surprising** / **makes people laugh** / **makes people feel sad**. (par. 2)

3. When something *mesmerizes* you, it is **boring** / **interesting** / **confusing**. (par. 2)

4. When people *indulge* you, they do something you **need** / **don't want** / **want**. (par. 3)

5. When you think something is *nonsense*, you don't **think it's meaningful** / **think it will happen** / **think it's reasonable**. (par. 4)

C Making Inferences

> Sometimes the reader must infer, or figure out, what the writer did not explain or state directly in the text.

Check (✓) the statements that you can infer from the reading.

___✓___ 1. Saturnina worked for the writer's family.

_____ 2. Señorita Luisa worked for the writer's family.

_____ 3. Señorita Luisa and the writer's mother were friends.

_____ 4. The writer's parents were born in a foreign country.

_____ 5. The writer's mother would be pleased that Saturnina had read wax for her daughter.

_____ 6. Unlike Señorita Luisa, the writer's mother wasn't superstitious.

D Relating Reading to Personal Experience

Discuss these questions with your classmates.

1. Do you believe in ghosts? Why or why not?

2. Were you more or less superstitious as a child than you are now? Do you still believe in superstitions? If so, which ones?

3. Have you ever gone to a fortune-teller? If so, did any of the predictions come true? If you have never gone to a fortune-teller, would you like to? Why or why not?

Lucky Hats and Other Fishing Superstitions

Thinking About the Topic

What do you know about fishing? Use the words in the box to complete the paragraph. Compare your answers with a partner.

| bait | boarding | catch | on board | overboard | school |

When you go fishing, the most important thing you need to bring _____ the
                                                                    1
boat is _____ because it's impossible to _____ fish without it. Before
              2   3
_____ the boat, you should also be sure to have a life jacket with you.
       4
If you're not wearing a life jacket and you fall _____, you could be in
                                                        5
trouble! Once you're out in the boat, you never know what's going to happen. The
last time I went fishing, there was a large _____ of bluefish, and I
                                                    6
went home with 18 of them. My wife wasn't happy. She hates bluefish.

Scanning

**Scan the reading to find and circle the words you wrote in the paragraph.
Then read the whole text.**

Last January, I was fortunate enough to go to Brazil on a fishing trip. As   1
we were boarding the vessel that would be our home for the next six nights,
I looked up and saw a huge bunch of ripe bananas hanging from a hook.

I was horrified. For more than 20 years, I have been told again and again   2
that bananas and boats just don't mix. I started talking about it with my
fishing companions. Not one had ever heard of such a superstition.

Yet just a few months earlier, I had read a paper about the banana   3
superstition. The author was unable to find its origin. One bit of
speculation is that dangerous creatures lurk inside the banana bunches. But
there's no doubt that anglers throughout the world believe that bananas
don't mix with fishing boats.

4   The bananas certainly didn't affect the fishing in Brazil. They were downright tasty, and the fishing was outstanding. But it got me to thinking about other superstitions regarding fishing.

5   For example, lucky hats. I had a lucky hat for a long time, a bright red cap that I was convinced was lucky. I caught a lot of fish – and a lot of big fish – wearing that hat. Then one day when I was angry, I threw it overboard. I'm convinced I haven't caught as many fish since.

6   Recently, a friend e-mailed me a list of "10 Fishing Superstitions" that appeared in a magazine. The lucky hat issue was addressed along with bananas. It says, "The 'right' hat can make or break a fishing trip, but it can't be one you bought yourself." Hmmm. Come to think of it, that lucky cap of mine was a freebie.

7   There also were some I'd never heard of. For example, rabbits crossing your path are bad luck. So are eggs.

8   One superstition we've all heard is that it's good luck to spit on your bait; but this particular list suggests that if the bait is a fish, you should kiss it. Actually, the idea of spitting on the bait probably has some merit. Just like a spray-on fish attractant, it can help disguise a smell that fish might find offensive.

9   There's also some merit in keeping the first fish you catch. Sheepshead fishermen, for example, don't like to release their fish[1] until they prepare to leave an area because it will scare the rest of the school.

10   I have a good friend who is convinced that he won't catch any fish unless he first spills a soft drink in his boat. You can't just pour the drink out; it has to be done accidentally. That means you need to leave the drink in a precarious position when you put it down.

11   There are other superstitions as well. If you catch a fish on the first cast, you might as well go home; it will be the only fish you will catch. Cameras on board are bad luck. (That's really tough for me.)

12   I'm sure there are plenty more superstitions out there, and I'd love to hear them. Let me know and I'll pass them along somewhere down the line. And remember, no bananas.

---

[1] These fishermen must follow rules about returning part of their catch to the sea to avoid reducing the sheepshead fish population.

Adapted from *The Post and Courier*

A Comprehension Check

Which events are good luck for fishermen, and which are bad luck? Check (✓) the correct column.

	Good Luck	Bad Luck
1. having bananas on a boat		
2. having rabbits cross in front of you		
3. having eggs on a boat		
4. spitting on bait		
5. spilling a soft drink on a boat		
6. catching a fish the first time you try		

B Vocabulary Study

Find the words in the reading that match these definitions.

1. boat _____ (par. 1)

2. idea about why something has happened _____ (par. 3)

3. hide and wait to jump out _____ (par. 3)

4. fishermen _____ (par. 3)

5. something you get for free _____ (par. 6)

6. benefit or advantage _____ (par. 8 & 9)

7. hide something _____ (par. 8)

8. not safe or stable _____ (par. 10)

C Understanding Pronoun Reference

▶ Writers use different kinds of pronouns to refer to information that is stated earlier in a text. Some common pronouns are *it* and *its*. Understanding pronoun reference is very important for reading comprehension.

What do these words refer to?

1. *it* (par. 2, line 2) _____

2. *its* (par. 3, line 2) _____

3. *it* (par. 4, line 2) _____

4. *it* (par. 5, line 3) _____

5. *It* (par. 6, line 2) _____

6. *it* (par. 6, line 3) _____

7. *it* (par. 8, line 2) _____

8. *it* (par. 10, line 2) _____

D Relating Reading to Personal Experience

Discuss these questions with your classmates.

1. Do you know any superstitions associated with sports other than fishing? If so, what are they?

2. Do you have a lucky hat (or other article of clothing)? If so, where did you get it? Why do you consider it lucky?

3. Who do you think are more superstitious – men or women? What examples can you give?

A Superstition About New Calendars

Predicting

Look at these statements from the reading. Find out the meanings of any words you don't know. Then answer the question below. Compare your answer with a partner.

1. . . . administrative assistants at work hand out new calendars in late November or early December.

2. . . . I'm likely to walk into a colleague's space and confront the offending object.

3. If I see one, I avert my eyes.

What do you think the writer's superstition is?

Skimming

Skim the reading to check your prediction. Then read the whole text.

1   Don't forget to throw that quarter into your pot of black-eyed peas tomorrow . . . for good luck, of course.

2   I picked up my share of superstitions growing up, and several of them are connected with the new year. The pot of peas seems more tradition to me than superstition, and it's easy to ignore since I don't cook. I can also say that another southern superstition – making sure a man is the first person to cross the threshold of your home on New Year's Day – also has no impact on my adult life. But one superstition I can't seem to escape is the one dealing with calendars. In my family, we believe it's bad luck to look at a new calendar before the start of the new year.

3   I can't ignore this because efficient administrative assistants at work hand out new calendars in late November or early December. And some of my co-workers hang them up as soon as they get them. So at any time, I'm likely to walk into a colleague's space and

confront the offending object. If I see one, I avert my eyes. Try as I might to rid myself of this superstition, I'm not willing to take any chances, either.

I go through the same contortions each December. What to do if I see a new calendar? How do I avert my eyes while still preserving the air of a professional? Sometimes it isn't easy. 4

I've found myself looking at the floor while talking with colleagues or studiously examining a spot on the wall far away from a new calendar. As yet, none of my co-workers has called me on my seeming aloofness. 5

This December when the administrative assistant at work asked if I wanted a calendar for next year, I didn't immediately say no as I usually do. I didn't say yes, either, but finally decided to rid myself of this silliness. So I did what any confident, competent adult does when confronted with a boogeyman of the past – I called my mother. 6

"Do you remember that superstition we had about putting a quarter in the black-eyed peas on New Year's Day?" I asked her. 7

"Well, it wasn't exactly a superstition," she said. "We did it for you kids. We wanted y'all to eat the peas, and maybe finding a quarter in your plate was just a way to get you to do it." 8

"You mean you were trying to bribe us to eat?" I asked incredulously. 9

"What about calendars?" I asked, finally getting to the point of my telephone call. "Have you ever heard that it's bad luck to look at a calendar before the New Year?" 10

"Not to look at it but to hang it," she replied. "It's bad luck to hang a new calendar before the New Year." 11

There it was. I had remembered my superstition wrong. My contortions were all for nothing. No more staring at my feet in the face of a new calendar. Looking at one wouldn't bring me bad luck. My co-workers who hung the calendars were going to have the bad luck! 12

Adapted from *The Washington Post*

A Comprehension Check

Mark each statement *T* (true) or *F* (false). Then correct the false statements.

<u>_F_</u> 1. The writer's family used to ~~eat~~ <u>throw a quarter into a pot of</u> black-eyed peas for good luck.

_____ 2. The writer used to think that if a man were the first to enter the home on New Year's Day, the family would have good luck.

_____ 3. The writer thought that if he waited until January to hang up a new calendar, he wouldn't have bad luck.

_____ 4. If colleagues were sitting near a new calendar, the writer would not look at the people while he was talking to them.

_____ 5. The writer called his mother to put an end to his superstition.

_____ 6. The actual superstition was not to look at a calendar before the new year.

B Vocabulary Study

Find these phrases in the reading. Then circle the letter of the correct meaning of each phrase.

1. *hand out new calendars* (par. 3)
   a. put calendars in people's hands
   b. give calendars to everyone

2. *walk into a colleague's space* (par. 3)
   a. meet a colleague
   b. go to a colleague's desk or office

3. *take any chances* (par. 3)
   a. believe in chance
   b. do anything risky

4. *I go through the same contortions each December.* (par. 4)
   a. I look up and down.
   b. I turn my body in unnatural ways.

5. *preserving the air of a professional* (par. 4)
   a. seeming professional
   b. not smoking in the office

C Summarizing

> When you summarize a text, you include only the most important information. A summary does not include details or examples. Summarizing is a strategy that can help you check your understanding of a text.

Cross out the sentences that don't belong in the summary.

Ever since he was a child, the writer had been superstitious about looking at a new calendar before January 1. He had other superstitions about the new year, too. His calendar superstition was a problem because some of his colleagues at work hung up new calendars in November or December. They hung them up as soon as they got them. The writer tried hard not to look at the calendars. It wasn't easy. Eventually, his mother told him that he had the superstition wrong: It was bad luck to hang up calendars before January 1, but it was fine to look at them. So it was his colleagues who would have the bad luck!

D Relating Reading to Personal Experience

Discuss these questions with your classmates.

1. Do you know any superstitions for other holidays? What are they?

2. Did your parents ever bribe you to do something? Do you think this is something parents should do? Why or why not?

3. Imagine a friend is worried that he is going to have bad luck because he broke a mirror. How would you help your friend put an end to this superstition?

> Reread one of the unit readings and time yourself. Note your reading speed in the chart on page 124.

UNIT 2 Health

Look at the titles of the readings and their brief descriptions to preview this unit's content. Before you begin each reading, answer the questions about it.

Reading 1

Diets of the World

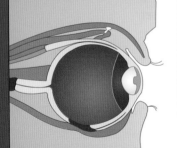

Why do people from some countries have fewer diet-related illnesses? This article from a Web site provides some answers.

1. What foods do you think are healthy to eat? What foods do you think are unhealthy?

2. What types of food do you associate with various countries? For example, which foods do you associate with China, Greece, and the United States?

3. What medical problems can result from unhealthy eating?

Reading 2

Drink, Blink, and Rest

In this magazine article, you can learn tips to help keep your eyes healthy.

1. Do you wear glasses or contact lenses? If so, how long have you worn them?

2. How many hours a day do you spend in front of either a television or a computer screen?

3. In the past few years, has your eyesight changed? If so, how?

Reading 3

Azeri Hills Hold Secret of Long Life

An unusually high number of people in Azerbaijan live to be over 100 years old. This magazine article explores some of the reasons.

1. What do you know about the country of Azerbaijan and the Azeri people?

2. What is the average life expectancy of men in your country? Of women?

3. What factors do you think lead to living a long life?

Diets of the World

Thinking About the Topic

Read the statements about diets of the world. Then check (✓) the place or places where you think each statement is true. Compare your answers with a partner.

	China	France	the Mediterranean	the United States
1. Lunch is the main meal of the day.				
2. Most of the fat is in the form of olive oil.				
3. The diet is primarily vegetarian.				
4. Meat is the focus of each meal.				
5. Shavings of meat are used only for flavoring.				
6. The diet is rich in green vegetables and fruit.				
7. The meals are eaten more slowly.				
8. Meals are high in saturated fat.				

Skimming

Skim the reading to see how your answers compare with what the writer says. Then read the whole text.

1   Why do people in Asia get a fraction of the cancer, heart disease, and diabetes that people in the United States get? Why are the French, with their rich sauces, so slim? The secret may simmer in their food. For intense flavor and a healthier body, come visit these diets of the world.

The Chinese diet

2   For centuries, the traditional Asian diet has been primarily vegetarian. For example, the Chinese diet typically features lots of vegetables, rice, and soybeans – and contains only shavings of meat for flavoring. This is far healthier than the traditional diet in the United States, which often features meat as the focus of the meal.

3   T. Colin Campbell, professor of nutrition at Cornell University, has compared the diets of the United States and rural China, where he tracked the eating habits of people living in 100 small villages. According to Campbell's research, the traditional Chinese diet consists of only 20 percent animal foods – far less than the amount in the typical American diet.

The French diet

Flaky croissants, frogs' legs swimming in butter, and chocolate mousse: Despite their rich diet, the French are generally slimmer than Americans. According to research, about 10 percent of the French qualify as obese, compared to over 30 percent of Americans. 4

How do the French do it? The French tend to snack less and savor their meals more slowly – which could lead to eating less food overall.

The eating patterns of the French offer significant clues to their healthfulness. For one, they traditionally don't take lunch lightly. In a study that tracked the eating habits of 50 workers in Paris and Boston, the French participants consumed 60 percent of their day's calories before 2 p.m., followed later by a small dinner, so they were less likely to sleep after eating the majority of their calories. Second, the study found that the French participants didn't snack, generally defined as consuming one to two between-meal foods. "The French ate less than one snack a day. Here in the United States, we have about three snacks a day," says R. Curtis Ellison, professor of preventive medicine at Boston University. 5

The Mediterranean diet

Ancel Keys was a scientist who lived to be 100 years old. When asked the secret of his long life, he explained that a typical night's meal would be baked cod flavored with lemon juice and olive oil, steamed broccoli, and roasted potatoes. 6

It's quintessentially Mediterranean, befitting the man who first promoted the health benefits of the Mediterranean diet. As a young scientist, Keys showed that among people in countries where fresh fruits and vegetables are plentiful and olive oil flows freely – Greece, southern Italy, southern France, parts of North Africa, and the Middle East – heart disease is rare. In countries where people fill their plates with beef, cheese, and other foods high in saturated fat – like the United States – it's a leading cause of death. 7

Key explains that the original Mediterranean diet, eaten by rural villagers on the Greek island of Crete, ". . . was nearly vegetarian, with fish and very little meat, and was rich in green vegetables and fruits." People living on Crete get more than one-third of their calories from fat, most of it from olive oil, which is rich in monounsaturated fatty acids. 8

Adapted from www.webmd.org

A Comprehension Check

Check (✓) the statement that best expresses the main idea of the reading.

_____ 1. Vegetarians live longer than meat eaters.

_____ 2. Your diet has a strong influence on your health.

_____ 3. People who travel should know about the diet of the country they visit.

_____ 4. The Mediterranean diet is the most healthful.

_____ 5. Saturated fat is bad for your health.

B Vocabulary Study

Find the words in *italics* in the reading. Then match the words with their meanings in the box.

| a. major | b. cause | c. contains | d. appropriate for |
| e. supported | f. observed | g. a small amount | h. taste or smell with pleasure |

_____ 1. *fraction* (par. 1)

_____ 2. *tracked* (par. 3)

_____ 3. *consists of* (par. 3)

_____ 4. *savor* (par. 4)

_____ 5. *lead to* (par. 4)

_____ 6. *befitting* (par. 7)

_____ 7. *promoted* (par. 7)

_____ 8. *leading* (par. 7)

C Identifying Main Ideas and Supporting Details

> Identifying the main ideas and supporting details in a text is an important strategy that will help your reading comprehension. It's a good idea to find the main ideas first. Then look for the supporting details that explain the main ideas more fully.

In the following list, find two main ideas from the reading and mark them *MI*. Find the details that support these main ideas and mark them *SD*. Then complete the sentences below by matching each *MI* with its two *SDs*.

_SD_ 1. For one thing, the French don't take lunch lightly.

_____ 2. According to Campbell's research, the traditional Chinese diet consists of only 20 percent animal foods – far less than the amount in the typical American diet.

_____ 3. The traditional Asian diet is primarily vegetarian.

_____ 4. The eating patterns of the French offer significant clues to their healthfulness.

_____ 5. For example, the Chinese diet typically features lots of vegetables, rice, and soybeans – and contains only shavings of meat for flavoring.

_____ 6. Second, the study found that the French participants didn't snack.

Sentence _____ is a main idea. It is supported by details _____ and _____.

Sentence _____ is a main idea. It is supported by details _____ and _____.

D Relating Reading to Personal Experience

Discuss these questions with your classmates.

1. Which eating habits discussed in the reading are similar to yours?

2. How would you describe the typical diet in your culture? In your family?

3. Think of your favorite meal. Which parts of the meal are healthy? Which are unhealthy?

Drink, Blink, and Rest

Thinking About What You Know

How much do you know about eyesight? Mark each statement *T* (true) or *F* (false). Compare your answers with a partner.

_____ 1. The sun can cause vision problems.

_____ 2. It is important to exercise your eye muscles.

_____ 3. You can only become nearsighted by inheriting the condition.

_____ 4. Constantly looking at computer screens can cause sore eyes.

_____ 5. Central heating and air conditioning make your eyes dry.

Skimming

Skim the reading to check your answers. Then read the whole text.

Our eyes are under a great deal of strain these days as computer work, television viewing, night driving, and even sunshine are making exceptional demands. Sunlight, especially in the summer, is now regarded as one cause of cataracts. 1

"The thinning of the ozone layer means more short-wave ultraviolet rays are reaching the earth, and these are the biggest risk factor for clouding the lens of the eye," says Jan Bergmanson, a Swedish optometrist. 2

Ultraviolet (UV) rays increase the risk of changes to the cornea – the outer shell of the eyeball – causing clouded vision and eventually cataracts. The rays can be shielded only by anti-UV lenses. However, our eyes are not sufficiently protected by fashion sunglasses. 3

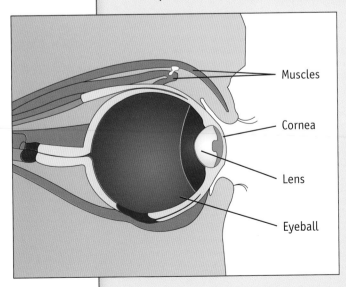

Muscles

Cornea

Lens

Eyeball

"Poor night vision and eye fatigue are noticeably more common, and there has been a big increase in minor eye complaints in the over-40s," says optometrist Dr. Mireille Bonnet, who took part in recent research. She says that the six muscles controlling each eye move more than 100,000 times a day and that everyone should learn to exercise their eye muscles and allow them to rest. 4

It was traditionally thought that near- or far-sightedness were inherited conditions and could not be influenced by environmental factors, but new research is challenging this assumption. 5

6   Recent studies suggest that up to 80 percent of schoolchildren in the United States and western Europe are nearsighted. Years of focusing on close, two-dimensional work causes most children to become at least slightly nearsighted by the age of 10, say the researchers.

7   Problems with night vision, which affect around 25 percent of people, are also on the increase because of computer use. Using computer screens means the eye must operate in electro-magnetic fields that make it work harder, and infrared from the screen adds to the strain. It is estimated that 25 to 30 percent of people have eye conditions, such as difficulty with night vision, that result from staring at a screen.

8   Concentrated visual work also slows down the rate of blinking, the process that washes the eyeball with tears and keeps it lubricated. At least 15 percent of people now suffer habitually from dry eyes, says Dr. Bonnet. Office workers are vulnerable because central heating and air conditioning dehydrate the tissues further, as does smoking. Keeping the eye moist has psychological benefits because dry eyes can make you feel tired.

9   There are two simple remedies to eyestrain: Drink more and blink more. Juan Duran, head of ophthalmology at Cruces Hospital in Bilbao, Spain, recommends closing the eyes for a minute every hour to rest them and retain their humidity. "An increasing number of people come to me with what they call tired eyes or eyestrain, and they sometimes complain of allergies. But the cause is very often dry eyes." Dryness also makes the eyes more susceptible to infection.

10   How to help your eyes:

- When doing close-up work, lift the eyes occasionally to focus on objects in the distance.
- When working on a computer, have a three-dimensional object on top and rest your eyes on it regularly.
- Close your eyes and rest them in the palms of your hands every hour or so.
- Do not stare at a screen or book: Blink more.
- Relax! Stress and tiredness have an immediate effect on our eyes, especially because they cause dryness.

Adapted from *The European Magazine*

A Comprehension Check

Check (✓) the three main ideas of the reading.

_____ 1. the effects of sunlight on the eyes

_____ 2. eye problems that are becoming more common

_____ 3. the reasons for an increase in eye problems

_____ 4. problems of office workers

_____ 5. fashion sunglasses

_____ 6. the best treatment for eyestrain

_____ 7. children's eye problems

_____ 8. the effects of computers on the eyes

B Vocabulary Study

Match the words from the reading that are similar in meaning.

_b_ 1. *protected* (par. 3)   a. *regarded* (par. 1)

____ 2. *thought* (par. 5)   b. *shielded* (par. 3)

____ 3. *work* (par. 7)   c. *fatigue* (par. 4)

____ 4. *keep* (par. 8)   d. *operate* (par. 7)

____ 5. *lubricated* (par. 8)   e. *moist* (par. 8)

____ 6. *vulnerable* (par. 8)   f. *retain* (par. 9)

____ 7. *tiredness* (par. 10)   g. *susceptible* (par. 9)

C Recognizing Cause and Effect

> In some texts, the reason why something happens (the cause) and what happens as a result (the effect) is important information and critical for your understanding of the whole text. Sometimes writers indicate cause and effect by using signal words or phrases, such as *causing, the cause, the result is,* or *resulting from / in.*

Circle the letter of the cause and effect sequence that describes the causes and effects that are mentioned in the reading. (→ = causes)

1. Paragraphs 2–3   a. UV rays → ozone layer thins → cataracts → clouded vision
                    b. ozone layer thins → UV rays → clouded vision and cataracts

2. Paragraph 6   a. nearsighted → more difficult to see close two-dimensional work
                    b. focus on close, two-dimensional work → become nearsighted

3. Paragraph 7   a. staring at a computer screen → eye conditions
                    b. eye conditions → electro-magnetic fields

4. Paragraph 9   a. allergies → infection
                    b. dryness → infection

D Relating Reading to Personal Experience

Discuss these questions with your classmates.

1. Have you experienced any of the eye problems described in the reading? If so, what have you done about them?

2. Which advice in the reading is the most helpful to you?

3. Do you wear sunglasses often? When do you wear them? Do you wear the kind with good UV protection?

Azeri Hills Hold Secret of Long Life

Predicting

Look at the picture and the title of the reading. Then check (✓) the reasons you think the Azeri villagers live long lives. Compare your answers with a partner.

_____ 1. hard work   _____ 3. fresh air   _____ 5. sense of humor

_____ 2. good doctors   _____ 4. herbal medicine   _____ 6. healthy diet

Skimming

Skim the reading to see which of your predictions the writer discusses. Then read the whole text.

1   You can see for kilometers from the mountains where Allahverdi Ibadov herds his small flock of sheep amid a sea of yellow, red, and purple wildflowers. The view from Amburdere in southern Azerbaijan toward the Iranian border is spectacular, but Mr. Ibadov barely gives it a second glance.

2   Why should he? He's been coming here nearly every day for 100 years.

3   According to his carefully preserved passport, Mr. Ibadov, whose birth was not registered until he was a toddler, is at least 105 years old. His wife, who died two years ago, was even older. They are among the dozens of people in this beautiful, isolated region who live extraordinarily long lives.

Mr. Ibadov's eldest son has just turned 70. He lost count long ago of how many grandchildren he has. "I'm an old man now. I look after the sheep, and I prepare the wood for winter. I still have something to do."

A lifetime of toil, it seems, takes very few people to an early grave in this region. Scientists admit there appears to be something in the Azeri mountains that gives local people a longer, healthier life than most.

Miri Ismailov's family in the tiny village of Tatoni are convinced that they know what it is. Mr. Ismailov is 110, his great-great-grandson is four. They share one proud boast: Neither has been to a doctor. "There are hundreds of herbs on the mountain, and we use them all in our cooking and for medicines," explained Mr. Ismailov's daughter, Elmira. "We know exactly what they can do. We are our own doctors."

There is one herb for high blood pressure, another for kidney stones, and a third for a hacking cough. They are carefully collected from the slopes surrounding the village. Experts from the Azerbaijan Academy of Science believe the herbs may be part of the answer. They have been studying longevity in this region for years. It began as a rare joint Soviet-American project in the 1980s, but these studies are not being funded any more.

Azeri scientists have isolated a type of saffron unique to the southern mountains as one thing that seems to increase longevity. Another plant, made into a paste, dramatically increases the amount of milk that animals are able to produce. "Now we have to examine these plants clinically to find out which substances have this effect," said Chingiz Gassimov, a scientist at the academy.

The theory that local people have also developed a genetic predisposition to long life has been strengthened by the study of a group of Russian émigrés whose ancestors were exiled to the Caucasus 200 years ago. The Russians' life span is much shorter than that of the indigenous mountain folk – though it is appreciably longer than that of their ancestors left behind in the Russian heartland.

"Over the decades, I believe local conditions have begun to have a positive effect on the new arrivals," Professor Gassimov said. "It's been slowly transferred down the generations."

But Mr. Ismailov, gripping his stout wooden cane, has been around for too long to get overexcited. "There's no secret," he shrugged dismissively. "I look after the cattle and I eat well. Life goes on."

Adapted from *Guardian Weekly*

A Comprehension Check

Mark each statement *T* (true) or *F* (false). Then correct the false statements.

_____ 1. Amburdere is a city in southern Azerbaijan.

_____ 2. Allahverdi Ibadov does not know exactly how old he is.

_____ 3. Mr. Ibadov can't do any kind of work anymore.

_____ 4. Miri Ismailov has never been to a doctor but his great-great-grandson has.

_____ 5. Elmira Ismailov is a doctor who uses herbs as medicines.

_____ 6. Scientists think people's genes might affect how long they live.

B Vocabulary Study

Find the words in *italics* in the reading. Then match the words with their meanings.

_____ 1. *toddler* (par. 3)   a. death at a young age

_____ 2. *toil* (par. 5)   b. the sides of a hill or mountain

_____ 3. *early grave* (par. 5)   c. made to leave one's own country

_____ 4. *slopes* (par. 7)   d. hard, physical work

_____ 5. *substance* (par. 8)   e. a very young child

_____ 6. *émigré* (par. 9)   f. a type of material

_____ 7. *exiled* (par. 9)   g. someone who leaves his or her country

C Understanding Pronoun Reference

> Writers use different kinds of pronouns to refer to information that is stated earlier in a text. Some common pronouns are *it, he, they, them,* and *that.* Understanding pronoun reference is very important for reading comprehension.

What do these words refer to?

1. *it* (par. 1, line 4)   _____

2. *They* (par. 3, line 3)   _____

3. *He* (par. 4, line 1)   _____

4. *they* (par. 6, line 1)   _____

5. *They* (par. 6, line 2)   _____

6. *them* (par. 6, line 4)   _____

7. *They* (par. 7, line 4)   _____

8. *that* (par. 9, line 4)   _____

D Relating Reading to Personal Experience

Discuss these questions with your classmates.

1. Would you like to live to be 105 years old? Why or why not?

2. Which type of medicine do you think works best: modern drugs or medicinal herbs? Explain your answer.

3. How old is the oldest person you know who is in good health? What do you think is the secret to his or her long life and health?

> Reread one of the unit readings and time yourself. Note your reading speed in the chart on page 124.

UNIT 3 Remarkable Talents

Look at the titles of the readings and their brief descriptions to preview this unit's content. Before you begin each reading, answer the questions about it.

Reading 1 ▶ ## The Memory Man

A prodigious memory is a rare talent. In this article, learn about an individual who became famous for the amazing things he could remember.

1. How would you describe your memory: excellent, reasonably good, or not very good?

2. What kinds of things do you remember easily? What do you have a hard time remembering?

3. What is the hardest thing you have ever had to memorize? Why was it hard?

Reading 2 ▶ ## Born to Paint: Alexandra Nechita

What happens to child prodigies after they become adults? Do they continue to develop, or do they lose interest in their passion? This article revisits one child prodigy 15 years after her name first appeared in the news.

1. Do you know of any child prodigies? What do you know about their lives?

2. What do you think are the advantages of being a child prodigy? What do you think are the disadvantages?

3. Would you describe yourself as artistic? Why or why not?

Reading 3 ▶ ## Hyper-polyglots

Imagine that you could speak 72 languages fluently, or even 10 or 20. The writer of this article examines the talent of hyper-polyglots, people who know more than a dozen languages.

1. Do you think hyper-polyglots can be equally fluent in all the languages they know? Why or why not?

2. Do you think people should try to learn as many languages as possible? Explain your answer.

3. In addition to the languages you already know, which languages would you like to learn? Why?

The Memory Man

Thinking About What You Know

Check (✓) the things you would like to be able to remember. Compare your answers with a partner.

_____ 1. every name and number in a telephone directory

_____ 2. every book that was read to you or that you have read

_____ 3. facts about history, literature, geography, and sports

_____ 4. the words and music to every song you have ever heard

_____ 5. every person you have ever met

Skimming

Skim the reading to find out which things Kim Peek, the subject of the reading, could remember. Then read the whole text.

1   Most of us have reasonably good memories. We are able to think back to different periods in our lives and remember where we were and things that happened then. But our memories are limited. For example, we cannot remember everyone we have ever met or what we did on every single day of our lives. And for most people, it would be impossible to read and remember every name and number in a telephone directory. Our brains simply do not allow us to retain such a vast amount of information.

2   However, there are some people who do have prodigious memories. These people have a rare condition known as savant syndrome. Savants suffer from a developmental disorder, but they also exhibit remarkable talents that contrast sharply with their

physical and mental disabilities. For example, a savant may exhibit brilliance in music, mathematics, or language learning but have great difficulty in other areas, as well as limited social skills.

Kim Peek (1951–2009) was a savant who lived in Salt Lake City, Utah, in the United States. He was born with damage to parts of his brain, but it seems that other parts of his brain – particularly those relating to memory – became overdeveloped to compensate. Peek's unique abilities emerged at a very early age. When he was just 20 months old, he could already remember every book that was read to him. After he had memorized a book, he would turn it upside down to show that he didn't need to read it again, and this became a life-long habit.

Peek could read two pages of a book at the same time – one page with the right eye and one with the left – in less than 10 seconds and remember everything he read. By the time he died, Peek had memorized more than 9,000 books. He could remember all the names and numbers in a variety of telephone books. He could recite thousands of facts about history, literature, geography, and sports. He could remember most classical music compositions and say when they were written and first performed as well as the dates of the composer's birth and death. Dr. David Treffert, an expert on savant syndrome, once described Peek as "a living Google" because of his astonishing ability to retain and connect facts. However, at the same time, Peek was unable to carry out simple tasks, such as brushing his hair or getting dressed, and he needed others to help him.

In 1989, the movie *Rain Man* won the Oscar for Best Picture. The main character in the movie, played by Dustin Hoffman, was based on Kim Peek's life. After this, people began to learn about Peek. He started to appear on television, where he would amaze audiences by correctly answering obscure questions on a range of topics. Peek became world famous, and he and his father began touring widely to talk about overcoming disabilities. For much of his life, Peek had been uncomfortable with people, but he began to enjoy sharing his experience, and his social skills improved. He inspired a great many people with his story and his words: "Recognizing and respecting differences in others, and treating everyone like the way you want them to treat you, will make our world a better place for everyone. You don't have to be handicapped to be different. Everyone is different!"

A Comprehension Check

Every paragraph in the reading has one main idea. Write the correct paragraph number for each main idea.

_____ a. This paragraph describes Kim Peek's interaction with people who wanted to know about his abilities.

_____ b. This paragraph explains what savant syndrome is.

_____ c. This paragraph describes Kim Peek's amazing memory for facts.

_____ d. This paragraph discusses what ordinary people are able to remember.

_____ e. The paragraph introduces Kim Peek and talks about his early talents.

B Vocabulary Study

Find the words in *italics* in the reading. Then match the words with their meanings.

_____ 1. *brilliance* (par. 2)   a. successfully dealing with something

_____ 2. *compensate* (par. 3)   b. covering a large area

_____ 3. *carry out* (par. 4)   c. difficult, out-of-the-ordinary

_____ 4. *obscure* (par. 5)   d. very high level of intelligence or skill

_____ 5. *widely* (par. 5)   e. perform a job or activity

_____ 6. *overcoming* (par. 5)   f. take the place of something useful or needed

C Reading Critically

> When you read critically, you don't just try to understand a text; you also react to it and evaluate it. In other words, you formulate an opinion about the content of the text.

Which of the following achievements in Peek's life impress you the most? Choose two. Then explain your choices to a partner.

- Peek could read two pages from a book in 10 seconds and remember everything in them.
- Peek's life was chosen as the inspiration for an award-winning movie.
- Peek had memorized 9,000 books by the time he died.
- Peek inspired people to accept their disabilities.
- Peek overcame his fear of meeting people and spoke to large audiences.

D Relating Reading to Personal Experience

Discuss these questions with your classmates.

1. If you could choose something to memorize – for example, a book, a song, a movie script – what would you choose? Explain your answer.

2. If there were a pill that you could take every day to allow you to remember everything, would you want to take the pill? Why or why not?

3. Have you ever been inspired by someone like Peek who had to overcome a disability? Who was it? How did that person inspire you?

Born to Paint:
Alexandra Nechita

Predicting

The reading tells about Alexandra Nechita in 1995 when she was 10 and also gives information about her in 2010 when she was 25. Read these five excerpts from the reading. Decide what year each excerpt describes. Write *1995* or *2010*.

_____ 1. She has been named Ambassador of Peace and Goodwill by the United Nations for her ongoing efforts to promote world peace through art.

_____ 2. Critics are comparing the work of this child prodigy to Picasso, Matisse, and other great artists.

_____ 3. She usually works in bronze and glass, and she has a particular interest in creating monumental pieces for public spaces.

_____ 4. She just seems to teach herself, and she has progressed quite naturally from crayons to pen and ink and then to oils and acrylics.

_____ 5. According to Alexandra, there isn't anything particularly special about her ability. It seems all very simple to her.

Skimming

Skim the reading to check your predictions. Then read the whole text.

1995

Ten-year-old Alexandra Nechita has been amazing the art world ever since she held her first exhibition at the age of eight. Critics are comparing the work of this child prodigy to Picasso, Matisse, and other great artists. Her colorful paintings sell for more than $50,000 each!   1

Alexandra was born in 1985 in Vaslui, Romania, and moved to the United States with her family two years later. Her artistic talent appeared very early when she began drawing at the age of two. The toddler spent every waking hour with her coloring books. At first her parents were worried that she would become introverted because she spent so much time drawing and painting. They took away the coloring books to encourage her to become interested in other things. But by the time Alexandra was seven, her parents decided to support her fascination with art, so they built a studio for her at home.   2

3   Alexandra has not had much formal art instruction. She just seems to teach herself, and she has progressed quite naturally from crayons to pen and ink and then to oils and acrylics. During the week, she normally spends three to four hours a day painting after school, and on weekends she often paints all day. But apart from her amazing talents as an artist, in the other areas of her life Alexandra is just like any other child of her age.

4   According to Alexandra, there isn't anything particularly special about her ability. It seems all very simple to her. "Every child has a talent or a gift," she says. "They can be the biggest of whatever they want to be. It takes dedication, determination, and perseverance. That's it."

5   Everyone wonders what this precocious 10-year old girl will be doing in the next 10, 15, or 20 years.

2010

6   Alexandra Nechita is a prolific 25-year-old artist. One art critic has described her as "possibly the most important female American artist of her day." Her work has been displayed all over the world, including the United Kingdom, France, Switzerland, Japan, the Netherlands, Italy, New Zealand, and Australia.

7   She prefers to paint in oils, and she paints on large canvases. She works quickly, and these days can complete several large paintings in a week. She paints in a style some describe as cubist, with large geometric shapes reminiscent of Picasso, and also with imaginative and dreamlike scenes that remind others of the painter Chagall. Alexandra's exceptional talent has led some people to call her "Mozart with a paintbrush."

8   Alexandra has also become a respected sculptor. She usually works in bronze and glass, and she has a particular interest in creating monumental pieces for public spaces. Just one example is her 16-foot sculpture, *Let There Be Peace*, which is on display at the Singapore Art Museum. In fact, peace is an important theme in much of Alexandra's work. She has been named Ambassador of Peace and Goodwill by the United Nations for her ongoing efforts to promote world peace through art.

A Comprehension Check

Answer the following questions with a partner.

1. Did Alexandra's parents encourage her to paint all the time when she was young?

2. How did Alexandra's parents help her?

3. How did Alexandra learn to draw and paint?

4. How are Alexandra's paintings as an adult different from her paintings as a child? How are they similar?

5. What new directions in art has Alexandra gone in since 1995?

6. What global issue is important to Alexandra?

B Vocabulary Study

Find the words or phrases in the reading that match these definitions. The number of blanks represents the number of words in the answer.

1. shy, quiet, and unable to make friends easily   _____ (par. 2)

2. showing unusually early mental development or achievement   _____ (par. 5)

3. producing a great number or amount of something   _____ (par. 6)

4. during the time when someone lived   _____ _____ _____ (par. 6)

5. making you remember a person or thing   _____ (par. 7)

6. unusually good   _____ (par. 7)

C Making Inferences

> Sometimes the reader must infer, or figure out, what the writer did not explain or state directly in the text.

Check (✓) the statements that you can infer from the reading.

____ 1. Alexandra was a good student in school.

____ 2. As a child, Alexandra didn't think she was different from other children.

____ 3. Alexandra's family wishes that she had not become a professional artist.

____ 4. Alexandra travels a lot.

____ 5. Alexandra has a lot of works of art to sell.

____ 6. Alexandra makes more money from her sculptures than from her paintings.

____ 7. Art will always be a part of Alexandra's life.

D Relating Reading to Personal Experience

Discuss these questions with your classmates.

1. Do you agree with Alexandra that people can be what they want to be if they have "dedication, determination, and perseverance"? Explain your answer.

2. Is there something you did as a child that you are better at now? How did you get better at it? Is there something you did that you are worse at now? Why?

3. If you could have one special talent, what would it be? Why?

Hyper-polyglots

Predicting

Look at the title, the art on this page, and the brief description of the reading on the first page of the unit. Then check (✓) the information you think you will find in the reading. Compare your answers with a partner.

_____ 1. different techniques for learning languages

_____ 2. astonishing language feats

_____ 3. brain research on hyper-polyglots

_____ 4. advice about how to learn languages on your own

_____ 5. the world's most widely spoken languages

_____ 6. a linguist's opinion on why some people are exceptional language learners

Skimming

Skim the reading to check your predictions. Then read the whole text.

1   Scientists have learned a great deal about how language ability can be impaired. We know, for example, how areas of the brain that are important for speech can be injured by a stroke or auto accident. But we don't know enough about what causes exceptionally strong language ability.

2   It's not unusual for people to speak two or three languages; they're known as bilinguals or trilinguals. Speakers of more than three languages are known as polyglots. And when we refer to people who speak many languages, perhaps a dozen or more, we use the term *hyper-polyglot*. Such people are known more through anecdotes than through science, but they do exist, and their language feats are astonishing.

3   The most famous hyper-polyglot was probably Giuseppe Mezzofanti, a nineteenth-century Italian cardinal, who was reputed to speak 72 languages. This claim sounds preposterous. If you assume each language had 20,000 words, Mezzofanti

would have to learn a word a minute, twelve hours a day, for five-and-a-half years – an impossible task. But Mezzofanti was tested by critics, and they were all impressed. Even if the stories are exaggerated, he was clearly a linguistic superstar.

Did Mezzofanti have an extraordinary brain? Or are hyper-polyglots just ordinary people with ordinary brains who manage to do something extraordinary through motivation and hard work? 4

U.S. linguist Stephen Krashen believes that exceptional language learners just work harder at it and have a better understanding of how they learn. As an example, he cites a Hungarian woman who worked as an interpreter during the second half of the twentieth century. When she was 86, she could speak 16 languages, including Chinese and Russian, and was still working on learning new languages. She said she learned them mostly on her own, reading fiction or working through dictionaries or textbooks. 5

Some researchers argue to the contrary. They believe that there is such a thing as a talent for learning languages and that there's something special about the actual brain of a hyper-polyglot. In the 1930s, a German neuroscientist examined parts of the preserved brain of a hyper-polyglot named Emil Krebs, who was said to have spoken 60 languages fluently. The scientist found that the area of Krebs's brain called Broca's region, which is associated with language, looked different from the Broca's region in the brains of 11 monolingual men. However, we still don't know if Krebs was born with a brain primed to learn languages or if his brain adapted to the demands he put on it. 6

How many languages can a person learn? In theory – except for having enough time to learn them – there's no limit to the human capacity for language. Everyone is potentially a polyglot, maybe even a hyper-polyglot. But if so, why are there so few people like Emil Krebs or Giuseppe Mezzofanti? Is it because hyper-polyglotism is simply a rare genetic trait? 7

Although it is still not clear whether the ability to learn exceptional numbers of languages is inborn, there's no doubt that just about all of us can acquire skills in a second, third, or even fourth language by putting our minds to it. It seems that monolinguals really have little excuse for not being able to speak another language. 8

Adapted from http://spinner.cofc.edu/linguist/archives/2005/11/?referrer=webcluster&

A Comprehension Check

Complete the chart with information about the people mentioned in the reading. Use a separate piece of paper if necessary. Compare your answers with a partner.

People mentioned in the reading	Their connection to the topic
1. Giuseppe Mezzofanti	
2. Stephen Krashen	
3. Hungarian woman	
4. German neuroscientist	
5. Emil Krebs	

B Vocabulary Study

Match the words from the reading that are similar in meaning.

_____ 1. *ability* (par. 1)   a. *impaired* (par. 1)

_____ 2. *injured* (par. 1)   b. *reputed* (par. 3)

_____ 3. *tested* (par. 3)   c. *extraordinary* (par. 4)

_____ 4. *exceptional* (par. 5) d. *examined* (par. 6)

_____ 5. *work harder* (par. 5) e. *capacity* (par. 7)

_____ 6. *said* (par. 6)   f. *put our minds to it* (par. 8)

C Recognizing Point of View

> Sometimes a writer expresses a point of view, or an opinion. An important part of reading critically is being able to recognize the presence of a point of view and determining what that point of view is.

Check (✓) the statement that best expresses the writer's point of view about language learners. Then compare your answer with a partner. Identify the parts of the reading that support your choice.

_____ 1. The brains of hyper-polyglots look different from those of monolinguals.

_____ 2. Exceptional language learners work harder than the rest of us and have a better understanding of how they learn.

_____ 3. More tests should be done to find out whether the ability to learn exceptional numbers of languages is inborn.

_____ 4. People can learn second, third, and fourth languages if they really want to.

D Relating Reading to Personal Experience

> Reread one of the unit readings and time yourself. Note your reading speed in the chart on page 124.

Discuss these questions with your classmates.

1. Which do you think is required to learn many languages, an extraordinary brain or motivation and hard work?

2. What is the most difficult problem for you in trying to learn a language? Explain your answer.

3. What techniques are especially helpful to you when you are learning a language?

UNIT 4 Beauty

Look at the titles of the readings and their brief descriptions to preview this unit's content. Before you begin each reading, answer the questions about it.

Reading 1 ▶ ## Executives Go Under the Knife

In this newspaper article, discover why more and more people in the workplace are turning to cosmetic surgery.

1. Do you know anyone who has had plastic surgery? If so, why did the person undergo the surgery?

2. How important do you think appearance is for success in business?

3. Do you think appearance is equally important for male and female executives? Why or why not?

Reading 2 ▶ ## What Makes a Man Attractive?

What features make a man handsome? In this newspaper article, you can learn about the surprising findings of some researchers.

1. What do you think makes someone attractive?

2. Do you think different cultures have the same ideas about beauty? Explain your answer.

3. How important do you think beauty is in choosing a mate?

Reading 3 ▶ ## In the Land of the Mirror

This magazine article takes a look at one country where glamour and winning beauty pageants are serious business.

1. Do you like to watch beauty pageants? Why or why not?

2. Are televised beauty pageants popular in your country?

3. Why do you think some women compete in beauty pageants?

Executives Go Under the Knife

Thinking About the Topic

Look at the pictures. Decide which descriptions below fit the people in the pictures. Write *1*, *2*, or *1 and 2* on the lines. Then compare your answers with a partner.

_____ looks like she has a lot of energy

_____ looks like she is ambitious

_____ looks like she might have low self-esteem

_____ looks like she might have difficulty getting ahead at work

Skimming

Skim the reading to see which woman would be less likely to get a promotion in the UK and why. Also, skim to see what that woman might do to increase her chances of getting a promotion.

1   A growing number of executives are investing in cosmetic plastic surgery to get ahead in the workplace, a research study has revealed.

2   Spending on cosmetic surgery in the United Kingdom has risen by more than a third, driven by the rising number of businesspeople – men and women – who are going under the knife to help them climb the career ladder.

3   The trend reflects frustration among a growing number of female executives who feel that a better physical appearance may finally help them break through the glass ceiling[1] in male-dominated companies.

4   Other businesspeople of both sexes fear that they may be replaced by younger, better-looking colleagues or be passed over for a promotion because their employers think they look tired or old.

---

[1] *glass ceiling:* an unofficial limit that prevents someone from advancing to a top position in the workplace

A report by Mintel, a market analysis firm, says, "A work culture which often equates 5
youth with energy and ambition, and maturity with irrelevance and lack of innovation, has
encouraged the use of cosmetic surgery by men and women to reduce signs of aging and so
improve their job prospects."

The report also points out that although to undergo plastic surgery for cosmetic reasons is 6
traditionally considered something that women do, male executives are starting to catch on to
its perceived advantages.

Nearly half of all working women questioned said they would consider having cosmetic 7
surgery, and nearly a fifth of female managers said they believed it would improve their
self-esteem.

Another study showed that among working women, plastic surgery is the third most 8
common reason for asking for a bank loan – after buying a car or paying for a vacation.

The director of a medical group that runs 10 cosmetic surgery clinics estimated that 9
about 30 percent of working women are having cosmetic surgery for reasons related to their
jobs. "There has been an increase in businessmen and businesswomen coming forward for
surgery," he said. "These are people that are perhaps a little older than their competitors in the
workplace and want to have as young-looking and attractive a face as possible. This is probably
of greater concern to men than women."

The director also said that women hoping to use cosmetic surgery to get ahead in business 10
tend to have facelifts, face peeling, laser skin resurfacing, and collagen replacement therapy.
Men tend to be more worried about the bags under their eyes.

According to the Mintel study, the biggest growth in spending has been on sub-surgical 11
procedures, most commonly used to reduce the appearance of facial wrinkles.

Despite the rise in work-related cosmetic surgery, not everyone is convinced that it's enough 12
to ensure success on the job. One experienced job consultant said: "Without doubt, looking
attractive is helpful in the workplace, but I do believe that someone with better skills and ability
will beat someone who only has good looks in an interview nine times out of ten. Your looks
might help you feel more confident, but they won't necessarily help you in your job."

Adapted from *The Scotsman*

A Comprehension Check

Complete each sentence with *men*, *women*, or *men and women*.

1. More _____ are undergoing cosmetic surgery than in the past.

2. _____ think that looking tired or old will cause them to lose
   their jobs.

3. Almost 50 percent of working _____ would consider having
   cosmetic surgery.

4. Almost 20 percent of _____ in management positions said cosmetic
   surgery would help them feel good about themselves.

5. _____ are probably more worried than _____ about
   younger-looking employees who have the same positions as they do.

6. The biggest worry for _____ is bags under the eyes.

B Vocabulary Study

Find the words or phrases in the reading that match these definitions. The number of blanks represents the number of words in the answer.

1. having an operation   _____ _____ _____ _____ (par. 2)

2. be successful at work   _____ _____ _____ _____ (par. 2)

3. not chosen   _____ _____ (par. 4)

4. employment opportunities   _____ _____ (par. 5)

5. experience something unpleasant   _____ (par. 6)

6. understand gradually   _____ _____ (par. 6)

7. almost always   _____ _____ _____ _____ _____ (par. 13)

C Summarizing

> When you summarize a text, you include only the most important information. A summary does not include details or examples. Summarizing is a strategy that can help you check your understanding of a text.

Find and underline three sentences below that would make a good summary of the reading.

More men and women are having cosmetic plastic surgery to help them get ahead in the workplace. One study shows they worry that they may not get ahead without plastic surgery. Many women executives feel a better appearance will help them get more top positions. Both men and women worry that if they look old and unattractive, they will lose their jobs or not get promoted. Many working women get a bank loan to pay for plastic surgery. The most popular procedure is to remove facial wrinkles. However, some experts think that people with better skills and ability will still do better than people who just look good.

D Relating Reading to Personal Experience

Discuss these questions with your classmates.

1. Would you consider having cosmetic surgery to help your career? Why or why not?

2. For which types of work do you think appearance is most important? Explain.

3. If you were a boss, would you hire someone because he or she was more attractive than someone else with the same skills? Explain your answer.

What Makes a Man Attractive?

Thinking About the Topic

Read the list of facial features, which are all from the reading. Look up any new words in a dictionary. Then check (✓) the features that you think people usually associate with handsome men. Compare your answers with a partner.

_____ 1. high cheekbones

_____ 2. thin lips

_____ 3. full lips

_____ 4. large nose

_____ 5. large jaw

_____ 6. small, deep-set eyes

_____ 7. wide eyes

_____ 8. heavy eyebrows

_____ 9. protruding forehead

_____ 10. delicate features

Skimming

Skim the reading to find out if most people agree with your answers. Then read the whole text.

You know it instinctively when you see the person walking toward you, or on a giant movie screen. A beautiful woman. A handsome man. Throughout the ages, a woman with delicate features, high cheekbones, full lips, and large, wide eyes has been considered a great beauty. For a man, the traditional assumption has been that the more rugged the appearance, the thicker the eyebrows, the thinner the lips, and the more deep-set the eyes, then the more attractive the man. Right?   1

According to some controversial research, not exactly. In a study published in the journal _Nature_, Scottish researchers report that both the men and women they studied found a slightly feminized male face more attractive.   2

The scientists found the preference appeared to hold true across three cultures surveyed: 92 men and women in Japan, South Africa, and Scotland picked more feminine male faces as the most handsome. "The finding came as a real surprise to us," said David   3

Perrett, a psychologist and one of the study's authors. "Individuals may differ in their preferences, but if you look at what the majority like, they chose the slightly feminized male face." The more masculine the face, the more the people studied associated it with coldness, dishonesty, and dominance. The feminized male face was seen as emotionally warm, someone who would be a faithful husband and a cooperative, loving father.

4   According to Perrett and his colleagues, how people perceive beauty has everything to do with how they choose their mates. Humans seek to preserve the species by producing the next generation. To ensure success, men tend to choose young women with delicate facial features who appear more likely to bear healthy children.

5   Women's choices are a bit more complicated. A number of previous studies show that some women clearly have preferred big, muscular men. As cavemen hunters in ancient times, they could provide the best food. Their physical strength meant their immune systems were robust and their genes good for producing healthy children. These men usually had protruding foreheads; heavy eyebrows; thin lips; small, deep-set eyes; and large noses and jaws.

6   However, Perrett and his colleagues refer to other studies showing this type of man was more likely to exhibit aggressive behavior. Thus, Perrett argues, women might be choosing men whose slightly feminized faces give the appearance that they'll be more likely to help raise the children.

7   Perrett's conclusions are already provoking debate. Not everyone in the growing field of "beauty research" agrees with the findings, although they do agree that the perception of beauty is a powerful influence on behavior.

8   One anthropologist who reviewed Perrett's study wondered why research about beauty should just apply to the face and not the body. "Ask women what they're looking for in a mate: Have they ever said shortness rather than tallness? Do they want shoulders a little narrower than average? I don't think so."

9   "From everything we know from science, from everyday experience, and from animal species about what makes a man attractive," the anthropologist continued, "I would not rush to conclude that women really like slightly feminine, nurturing daddies for mates."

Adapted from *The Gazette*

A Comprehension Check

Look at the example. Then find and correct seven more mistakes in this paragraph.

Researchers in ~~Japan~~ Scotland interviewed men and women in two countries. They found that both men and women prefer masculine male faces. Psychologist David Perrett was not surprised about the findings. He says people see masculine faces and think of emotional warmth, dishonesty, and dominance; however, when they see feminine faces, they think of coldness, faithfulness, and cooperation. According to Perrett, in ancient times, men chose women who seemed likely to provide healthy food, while women chose men for less complicated reasons.

B Vocabulary Study

Find the words in the box in the reading. Then complete the sentences.

instinctively (par. 1)	rugged (par. 1)	controversial (par. 2)
slightly (par. 2)	aggressive (par. 6)	nurturing (par. 9)

1. Tom and his brother Hank look very similar, but Tom is _____ taller.

2. The book is _____. Many readers disagree with the writer's ideas.

3. There are certain things we do _____, without thinking about them.

4. She was a great mother, warm and _____.

5. His face was not smooth or soft. It had a _____ quality.

6. You have to be _____ if you want to succeed in business.

C Understanding Text Organization

> In a well-organized text, related topics are grouped together and presented in a logical sequence. If you understand how a text is organized, it will be easier to understand the ideas.

Write the correct paragraph number or numbers next to each topic from the reading. (Note: You will use each paragraph number once.)

a. __2, 3__ conclusions from Perrett's study

b. _____ the state of the current debate about what makes men attractive

c. _____ common assumptions about beauty

d. _____ how men choose women who will be good mates

e. _____ how women choose men who will be good mates

Now complete the diagram with the correct letters to see the logical sequence of ideas.

D Relating Reading to Personal Experience

Discuss these questions with your classmates.

1. Do you agree with Perrett's findings? What examples can you give?

2. Which famous people do you think are good-looking? Describe their facial features.

3. Think of two or three men you know. Are their faces "masculine" or "slightly feminized"? Do their personalities match their facial features? Explain your answer.

In the Land of the Mirror

Predicting

This reading was written by a journalist in Venezuela. Look at the title and the picture. Then check (✓) the information you think you will find in the text. Compare your answers with a partner.

_____ 1. Venezuela has won more international beauty pageants than any other country.

_____ 2. It costs a lot of money to enter beauty pageants.

_____ 3. Experts change women's appearance in order to win beauty pageants.

_____ 4. Contestants get help from dermatologists, dietitians, and plastic surgeons.

_____ 5. Many Venezuelans criticize their country's interest in beauty pageants.

_____ 6. Venezuela leads Latin America in spending on cosmetics.

Skimming

Skim the reading to check your predictions. Then read the whole text.

1   In much of Latin America, soccer is the popular passion, but here it is beauty pageants. Everyone, it seems, knows the Miss Venezuela anthem, and the finale in September is the top-rated TV show. Though a nation of just about 27 million, Venezuela is a beauty-pageant superpower.

2   In the past 30 years, it has won the crown nine times in the top two contests, Miss Universe and Miss World, which is more than any other country. Locals credit their melting pot of backgrounds – European, African, and Indian –with producing one knockout after another. But the real reason has more to do with applying industrial-type efficiency to turning out beauty queens.

3   The undisputed captain of that industry is Osmel Sousa, the head of the Miss Venezuela Organization. He and his scouts comb malls, universities, and beaches for the

"rough diamonds" who will be cut and polished to near perfection – by his definition, anyway. Sousa has help from more than 20 specialists: plastic surgeons, dentists, dermatologists, dietitians, hair and makeup experts, personal trainers, and psychologists. He looks at women the way a sculptor views a piece of clay: "I mold the person," he says proudly. "I derive my enjoyment by changing the women for the better. Otherwise, it would be a bore."

Skin too light or too dark? Creams can handle that. Gummy smile or biggish nose? Surgery can remake it. Appraisals can be harsh. "Oh my, she has too much chin and her lips are too big!" gasps dermatologist Sonia Roffe, as one contestant struts by. "We'd have to fix that." 4

The wannabe Misses regard Sousa's glamour factory as a ticket to the good life. "This organization can launch my career," says Ilana Furman, who has wanted to be a Miss since she was a child. "It's the dream of all Venezuelan girls." Still, she has some anxiety. "Osmel said I have a thick nose," she frets. "I told the organization I don't want them to touch my face. . . . I hope they can fix it with cosmetics." 5

Workouts. The fitness and food regimen is tough. Margie Rosales, a college communications major, was a winner in the Caracas casting but admits that daily six-hour gym workouts and a menu of chicken breasts, egg whites, and seaweed can get her down. "I was depressed because the diet was really hard," she says. "I've put a lot into this." 6

Other Venezuelans put a lot into looks, too. This nation leads Latin America in per capita spending on cosmetics. A Roper Starch Worldwide poll of 30 countries found that Venezuelans are the vainest of them all: Sixty-five percent of women and 47 percent of men said they think about their looks "all the time." 7

Here in Beauty Land, schools and clubs pick beauty queens from an early age. Doting fathers give their daughters a nose job for their sixteenth birthday. Astrid Cabral, an accounting student visiting a hair salon, says she plans to have plastic surgery to heed her boyfriend's call to "be like a Miss." Says Cabral, "It's more important to be smart, but the sad fact is that women in Venezuela are forced to concentrate on their own beauty because men demand it." 8

Adapted from *U.S. News & World Report*

A Comprehension Check

Check (✓) the statement that best expresses the main idea of the reading.

_____ 1. Osmel Sousa is the most important person in the beauty pageant business.

_____ 2. Venezuelan women think they can have a good life if they win a beauty pageant.

_____ 3. Although Venezuelan women who enter beauty pageants want to look better, some of them don't want to have plastic surgery.

_____ 4. Venezuelans are very serious about beauty pageants, and they put a lot of effort into winning them.

_____ 5. Many Venezuelan women undergo plastic surgery, difficult fitness regimens, and diets in order to win beauty pageants.

B Vocabulary Study

Find the words in *italics* in the reading. Then match the words with their meanings.

_____ 1. *knockout* (par. 2)   a. judgments

_____ 2. *appraisals* (par. 4)   b. the most proud about appearance

_____ 3. *harsh* (par. 4)   c. cruel, unkind

_____ 4. *gasps* (par. 4)   d. showing a lot of love

_____ 5. *struts* (par. 4)   e. walks in a proud way

_____ 6. *launch* (par. 5)   f. a very attractive woman

_____ 7. *vainest* (par. 7)   g. begin

_____ 8. *doting* (par. 8)   h. says something while taking in a short quick breath

C Understanding Pronoun Reference

> Writers use different kinds of pronouns to refer to information that is stated earlier in a text. Some common pronouns are *it, he, his, her, they*, and *them*. Understanding pronoun reference is very important for reading comprehension.

What do these words refer to?

1. *it* (par. 1, line 1)   _____

2. *his* (par. 3, line 3)   _____

3. *He* (par. 3, line 6)   _____

4. *it* (par. 4, line 2)   _____

5. *them* (par. 5, line 4)   _____

6. *they* (par. 7, line 4)   _____

7. *her* (par. 8, line 4)   _____

8. *it* (par. 8, line 6)   _____

D Relating Reading to Personal Experience

Discuss these questions with your classmates.

1. How much do you think about your looks: a lot, a little, or not at all?

2. What is your opinion about beauty pageants? Do you approve of them? Why or why not?

3. What would you advise a young girl to do who wanted to compete in beauty pageants?

> Reread one of the unit readings and time yourself. Note your reading speed in the chart on page 124.

5 Technology

Look at the titles of the readings and their brief descriptions to preview this unit's content. Before you begin each reading, answer the questions about it.

Reading 1 ▶

Affectionate Androids

What will the future relationships between humans and robots be like? In this newspaper article, find out what researchers are saying.

1. What are robots used for nowadays?

2. If you had a robot at home, what would you want it to do for you?

3. What attributes, or features, do humans have that robots could never have?

Reading 2 ▶

Identification, Please!

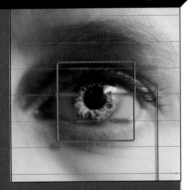

This Internet article looks at modern technologies that can verify, or prove, a person's identity.

1. How often do you use a password or PIN (personal identification number) to prove your identity?

2. What problems do people sometimes have with passwords or PINs?

3. What do you think is the best way to verify someone's identity?

Reading 3 ▶

Researchers Worry as Cyber-teens Grow Up

In this newspaper article, the writer describes some problems that result when adolescents spend a lot of time online and texting.

1. What hobbies are good for teenagers? Which could be harmful?

2. Where do teens like to spend time in your city or town? Are there any special hangouts? Give examples.

3. Is spending time on the Internet good for teens? Why or why not?

Affectionate Androids

Thinking About the Topic

The topic of the reading is robots. Check (✓) the sentences you think are true about robots nowadays. Compare your answers with a partner.

_____ 1. Robots can giggle.

_____ 2. Robots can be tickled.

_____ 3. Robots can play with children.

_____ 4. Robots can dress themselves.

_____ 5. Robots can recognize faces and voices.

_____ 6. Robots can eat and drink.

Skimming

Skim the reading to check your answers. Then read the whole text.

1   Computers are now powerful enough to allow the age of humanoid robots to dawn. And it won't be long before we will see realistic cyber companions, complete with skin, dexterity, and intelligence. They will be programmed to tend to your every need.

2   Will we ever want to marry robots? Artificial intelligence researcher David Levy has published a book claiming human-robot relationships will become popular in the next few decades. And if you want to go ahead and tie the knot with your special electronic friend, Levy said that such marriages will be socially acceptable by around 2050.

3   Will humans really be able to form deep emotional attachments to machines? It will, in fact, be relatively easy to form these strong attachments because the human mind loves to anthropomorphize: to give human attributes to other creatures – even objects.

4   For example, researchers in San Diego recently put a small humanoid robot in with a toddler playgroup for several months. The bot knew each child because it was

programmed with face and voice recognition, and it giggled when tickled. The children ended up treating it as a fellow toddler. When it lay down because its batteries were flat, the kids even covered it with a blanket.

In a few decades, when humanoid robots with plastic skin look and feel very real, will people want to form relationships with them? What if the bots could hold a conversation? And be programmed to be the perfect companions – soul mates, even? Maybe your generation could resist, but eventually there will be a generation of people who grow up with humanoid robots as a normal part of life. And like those toddlers in the experiment, they will be very accepting of them. **5**

The next question, then, is whether there is anything wrong with having an emotional relationship with a machine. Even today there are people who form deep attachments to their pets and use them as substitutes for friends or even children. Few consider that unethical. **6**

But a sophisticated robot will probably be even more attractive. For those who always seem to end up marrying the wrong man or woman, a robotic Mr. or Ms. Right could be mighty tempting. As the father of artificial intelligence, Marvin Minsky, put it when asked about the ethics of lonely older people forming close relationships with robots: "If a robot had all the virtues of a person and was smarter and more understanding, why would the elderly bother talking to other grumpy old people?" **7**

A robot could be programmed to be as dumb or smart, as independent or subservient, as an owner desired. And that's the big disadvantage. Having the perfect robot partner will damage the ability to form equally deep human–human relationships. People will always seem imperfect in comparison. When you're behaving badly, a good friend will tell you. However, few owners will program their robots to point out their flaws. **8**

People in relationships have to learn to adapt to each other: to enjoy their common interests and to deal with their differences. It makes us richer, stronger, and wiser. A robot companion will be perfect at the start. However, there will be nothing to move the relationship to grow to greater heights. **9**

Adapted from *Sunday Age*

A Comprehension Check

The writer asks the following questions. Circle the letter of the correct answer.

1. Will we ever want to marry robots?
   a. One researcher claims that we will be doing so by around 2050.
   b. No, people won't ever think it's a good idea to marry robots.

2. Will humans really be able to form deep emotional attachments to machines?
   a. Yes, they will because experiments have shown that they already do so.
   b. It's clear that children will be able to form attachments, but probably not adults.

3. Is there anything wrong with having an emotional relationship with a machine?
   a. Such a relationship could make people happier, so there is nothing wrong with it.
   b. It is not really wrong, but it will harm human–human relationships.

B Vocabulary Study

Match the words from the reading that are similar in meaning.

_____ 1. *androids* (title)

_____ 2. *tie the knot* (par. 2)

_____ 3. *attachments* (par. 3)

_____ 4. *unethical* (par. 6)

_____ 5. *mighty* (par. 7)

_____ 6. *tempting* (par. 7)

_____ 7. *put it* (par. 7)

_____ 8. *close* (par. 7)

a. *relationships* (par. 2)

b. *robots* (par. 1)

c. *marry* (par. 2)

d. *said* (par. 2)

e. *strong* (par. 3)

f. *very* (par. 5)

g. *wrong* (par. 6)

h. *attractive* (par. 7)

C Identifying Main Ideas and Supporting Details

> Identifying the main ideas and supporting details in a text is an important strategy that will help your reading comprehension. It's a good idea to find the main ideas first. Then look for the supporting details that explain the main ideas more fully.

In the following list, find two main ideas from the reading and mark them *MI*. Find the details that support these main ideas and mark them *SD*. Then complete the sentences below by matching each *MI* with its three *SD*s.

_____ 1. There will be problems if human–robot relationships become popular in the future.

_____ 2. In one experiment, toddlers played with a robot and treated it as another child.

_____ 3. Human–human relationships won't grow stronger.

_____ 4. People won't learn how to adapt to each other and deal with their differences.

_____ 5. People will always seem imperfect to each other in comparison with robots.

_____ 6. The human mind loves to give human attributes to other creatures and objects.

_____ 7. The kids even covered the robot with a blanket when its batteries died.

_____ 8. It's easy for humans to form strong attachments to animals and objects.

Sentence _____ is a main idea. It is supported by details _____, _____, and _____.

Sentence _____ is a main idea. It is supported by details _____, _____, and _____.

D Relating Reading to Personal Experience

Discuss these questions with your classmates.

1. Do you think human–robot relationships will be common by 2050? Why or why not?

2. Do you think it would be harder or easier to have a robot companion instead of a human friend? Explain your answer.

3. What qualities would you like a robot friend to have?

Identification, Please!

Previewing Vocabulary

The words in the box are from the reading about biometrics technology. Discuss the meanings of the words with a partner. Look up any new words in a dictionary. Then discuss what *biometrics technology* probably means. Write a definition.

iris scan	stored image
voice scan	fingerprint scan
identity verification	embedded cameras
physiological and/or behavioral characteristics	stored file

biometrics technology: _____

Scanning

Scan the reading to find the writer's definition. Then read the whole text.

"Iris scan, please," the bank's computer voice tells you. You step up and the computer   1
reads your eye, comparing it to the stored file it has of your iris. The images had better
match – otherwise, you won't be able to get your money.

Iris scanning and other technologies, such as fingerprint and voice scanning, have   2
appeared in many science fiction movies in the past. Today, these advanced technologies
are part of the real world. They are prevalent at work, the bank, the airport, and your
local prison. The iris scan, fingerprint scan, and voice scan are all examples of biometrics,
a fast developing area of automatic personal identification technology. Basically,
biometrics uses various means to verify a person's identity, based on the individual's
unique physiological or behavioral characteristics. Biometric tests generally capture an
image on camera, compare it to a stored image, and check for characteristics that match.

3   Biometrics technologies can be used to verify fingerprints, voices, irises, body heat patterns, facial images, handprints, signatures, and even computer keystroke rhythms. To increase accuracy, several different verification systems can be employed. Biometrics verification is currently in use in some airports, prisons, and hospitals to help control access to restricted areas. It is also being used by law enforcement and government agencies.

4   Biometrics identification systems have a number of advantages over password or PIN (personal identification number) systems. The primary advantage is that an individual has to be physically present in order to be identified. Another important advantage is that there are no passwords to remember, forget, forge, lose, or steal.

5   Biometrics technology is now much more accessible, mainly because the costs of implementing the technology are plummeting. Many companies have begun to adopt biometrics identification systems, including scanners and embedded cameras, to give their large computer networks stronger security than simple password systems can provide.

6   The voice scan is the simplest and most affordable form of biometrics. All that is required is a computer, a microphone, and the correct software. The software records a subject's voice and then compares it with a stored voice sample for identification purposes.

7   For additional security, fingerprint and handprint scans can also be employed. Fingerprint scans capture the image of a fingerprint and compare it to a stored file of prints. Handprint scans capture the unique geometric features of a hand.

8   Iris scans currently give the highest level of accuracy among all the available biometrics systems. Another technology, full facial scans, is currently in use at border crossings and airports. Facial scanning equipment can actually track and identify moving faces within a crowd.

9   The potential of biometrics is exciting and encouraging. With continued development, testing, and application, current technologies will become even more effective in the future. Soon, the days of car keys, passwords, and PINs will be gone. Just don't leave home without your fingerprints!

Adapted from *NetWeek*

A Comprehension Check

Mark each statement _T_ (true) or _F_ (false). Then correct the false statements.

_____ 1. Biometrics technology is not in use now.

_____ 2. Biometrics technology can measure many different things.

_____ 3. Fingerprint and handprint scans are done the same way.

_____ 4. All biometrics technologies are equally accurate.

_____ 5. Biometrics technology verifies identity more accurately than passwords and PINs.

_____ 6. Biometrics technology uses stored information to verify identity.

B Vocabulary Study

Find the words in *italics* in the reading. Then circle the correct meaning of each word.

1. When something is *prevalent*, it is **common** / **real** / **unusual**. (par. 2)

2. If something is *unique*, it is **the only one** / **one of many** / **very popular**. (par. 2)

3. A technology that is *accessible* is **easy to get** / **difficult to get** / **unlikely to fail**. (par. 5)

4. When you *implement* new technology you **use** / **change** / **increase** it. (par. 5)

5. When costs *plummet*, they **increase** / **decrease** / **stay the same**. (par. 5)

6. If something has good *potential*, it **has succeeded** / **is succeeding** / **will probably succeed**. (par. 9)

C Recognizing Purpose

> Writers create texts for different purposes. For example, sometimes a writer wants to give information. Other times, the writer wants to persuade the reader to do something. Recognizing a writer's purpose will help you better understand what you read.

Check (✓) the writer's main purpose in the reading. Discuss the reasons for your answer with a partner.

_____ 1. to compare biometrics with other identification technologies

_____ 2. to discuss the pros and cons of biometrics technology

_____ 3. to inform people about biometrics technology

_____ 4. to persuade people to put money into biometrics technology

D Relating Reading to Personal Experience

Discuss these questions with your classmates.

1. Which biometrics identification systems are used in your country? Where are they used?

2. What are the advantages of biometrics technology? What are the disadvantages?

3. Do you think biometrics identification systems should not be used in certain places (for example, schools, workplaces, apartment buildings, banks, hospitals, airports)? Why or why not?

Researchers Worry as Cyber-teens Grow Up

Predicting

Look at the title of the reading and the picture. Check (✓) the worries you think you will read about in the text. Compare your answers with a partner.

_____ 1. problems teens have in developing interpersonal relationships

_____ 2. problems of teen violence that result from online activities

_____ 3. concerns of researchers about teens' computer habits

_____ 4. effects of online activities on the health of teens

_____ 5. problems teens have doing homework

Skimming

Skim the reading to check your predictions. Then read the whole text.

1   Teens don't understand the big fuss. Growing up in a technological world, they have had computers around them all their lives. And they love to spend hours chatting online and texting their friends. So what?

2   But researchers are increasingly concerned that, as cyberspace replaces the pizza parlor as the local hangout, adolescents are becoming more isolated and less adept at forming interpersonal relationships. Researchers are asking what will happen to teens in the future, when so many of them are spending hours on the Internet, with little face-to-face contact.

"We're not only looking at what the computer can do *for* us, but what they are doing *to* us," said sociologist Sherry Turkle. "It's on so many people's minds." She wants to know how a teen's sense of self and values may be altered by the Internet, where there are no limits to making personal connections and creating new identities.

Social psychologist Robert Kraut said he's concerned about the "opportunity costs" of spending so much time online. He found that teens who used computers, even just a few hours a week, showed increased signs of loneliness and social isolation. In his study of 100 families that use the Internet, Kraut said that the teens reported having fewer friends to socialize with, possibly because their computer time replaced hours they would have spent with others. "Chatting online may be better than watching television, but it's worse than hanging out with real friends," he said.

Today's teens, however, don't see anything strange in the fact that the computer screen occupies a central place in their social lives. "School is stressful and busy. There's almost no time to just hang out," said Parker Rice. "Talking online is just catch-up time."

Many teens acknowledge that there's an unreal quality to their cyberspace communication, including their odd shorthand terms, such as POS (parent over shoulder) or LOL (laughing out loud). Psychologists see this code of communicating as part of the exclusive shared language that teenagers love.

Teens don't seem to expect the online world to be the same as the real world. They aren't surprised when someone, who is only an acquaintance, shares a personal secret. They also show a remarkable tolerance for people who don't tell the exact truth. For example, Jonathon Reis wasn't put off when he learned that a girl wasn't totally honest when she described herself online. "I know it's likely they'll say they look better than they do," he said.

Teens say they appreciate the fact that they can take the time to think about a response to an e-mail or a text message. Some teens admit that asking someone for a date, or breaking up, can be easier in message form. But they say there's nothing wrong with this, and cyberspace has become just another medium – like the telephone – in the world of adolescence.

Adapted from *The Boston Globe*

A Comprehension Check

Every paragraph in the reading has one main idea. Write the correct paragraph number for each main idea.

_____ a. A sociologist asks what the online world teaches teens about themselves.

_____ b. Teens use special language online.

_____ c. Communicating online is important in a teen's social life.

_____ d. Researchers are concerned about the future effects of online use on teens.

_____ e. Teens see advantages in not talking to someone directly.

_____ f. The lack of honesty online does not bother teens.

_____ g. Teens think it's OK to spend many hours online or texting.

_____ h. A psychologist is concerned about loneliness among teens.

B Vocabulary Study

Find the words in *italics* in the reading. Then match the words with their meanings.

_____ 1. *fuss* (par. 1)   a. written with abbreviations and symbols

_____ 2. *isolated* (par. 2)   b. a way of communicating information to people

_____ 3. *adept* (par. 2)   c. separated and alone

_____ 4. *odd* (par. 6)   d. bothered or discouraged by something

_____ 5. *shorthand* (par. 6)   e. a lot of unnecessary worry

_____ 6. *exclusive* (par. 6)   f. skillful

_____ 7. *put off* (par. 7)   g. unusual or strange

_____ 8. *medium* (par. 8)   h. limited to one group of people

C Making Inferences

> Sometimes the reader must infer, or figure out, what the writer did not explain or state directly in the text. For example, it is often possible to make inferences about people's opinions.

Make inferences about opinions, based on the information in the text. Mark each sentence as researcher's opinion (R) or teenager's opinion (T).

_R_ 1. Spending a lot of time online affects teenagers' ability to form relationships.

_____ 2. Teens who use computers to chat have fewer friends.

_____ 3. There's nothing wrong with teens spending hours online.

_____ 4. Every hour that teens are online is one hour less they could spend with a friend.

_____ 5. The Internet provides a great way to keep in touch with friends.

_____ 6. It's all right for people not to be completely honest when they're online.

_____ 7. It's good to have more time to think about what to say online.

_____ 8. Teens might be developing a different sense of what's right and wrong.

D Relating Reading to Personal Experience

Discuss these questions with your classmates.

> Reread one of the unit readings and time yourself. Note your reading speed in the chart on page 124.

1. Do you think today's teens spend too much time online? Why or why not?

2. Do you think that everything can be communicated by e-mail or texting? Or are some things best said face-to-face? Explain your answer and give examples.

3. Would it bother you if people lied to you online about their age or appearance? Why or why not?

UNIT 6 Punishment

Look at the titles of the readings and their brief descriptions to preview this unit's content. Before you begin each reading, answer the questions about it.

Reading 1 › Spanking on Trial

A man from the United States on vacation in Canada spanked his daughter because she was disobedient and behaving badly. This magazine article tells what happened to him and why.

1. Is spanking a common punishment in your culture? If not, how do parents punish children when they are misbehaving?

2. Have you ever been spanked or seen anyone being spanked? What was your reaction?

3. Do you think there should be laws to protect children from parental punishment? Why or why not?

Reading 2 › The Letter

In this excerpt from a novel, a girl gets into trouble with her mother because of a letter.

1. Have you ever angered your parents? If so, how?

2. Have your parents ever disapproved of your friends? If so, what did you do about it?

3. Have your parents ever asked you to do something you didn't want to do? If so, what happened?

Reading 3 › Schools Take the Fun Out of Suspension

How is school suspension changing? This newspaper article looks at ways some California schools are dealing with students who misbehave.

1. Do schools in your community suspend students? If not, how are students punished for bad behavior?

2. In your community, is cleaning the school a duty or a punishment?

3. If you were a parent, how do you think you would react if your child was suspended or punished by the school?

Spanking on Trial

Previewing Vocabulary

Each of the following sentences from the reading contains an idiom. Discuss with a partner what you think each idiom means.

1. Rachel was acting up, refusing to stop wrestling with her brother. (*act up*)

2. Rachel went over the line. She pushed her brother out of the car. (*go over the line*)

3. "We were just passing through . . . and we found ourselves in big trouble." (*pass through*)

4. "To have the person you are most dependent on turn on you is a psychological blow." (*turn on*)

Scanning

Scan the reading to find the idioms. Check the contexts to see if your definitions are correct. Then read the whole text.

1   It was his wife's birthday, and David Peterson took a break on the drive home from a vacation in Canada to celebrate the occasion at a restaurant in London, Ontario. The whole family was with him – wife Paula, five-year-old daughter Rachel, and son William, two. But Rachel was acting up, refusing to stop wrestling with her brother. When Peterson and his kids went back to the car to get the present they had for their mother, Rachel went over the line. She pushed her brother out of the car. Then she slammed the door on his fingers when he tried to get back in. Angered, Peterson did what parents have done with insolent children for centuries: He spanked her. But Marlene Timperio, the mother of a six-year-old boy, saw it all. Noting the Illinois license plate on his vehicle, Timperio confronted the American, telling him, "This is not what we do in Canada." And then she called the police.

2   So began David Peterson's ordeal, which included a night in a London jail and months of legal headaches, culminating in his trial and acquittal on charges of assault. "We were just passing through," he told reporters after the verdict in London, "and we found ourselves in big trouble."

3   Indeed. There are few more contentious issues in parenting – to spank or not to spank? And the Peterson case has only added fuel to the long-standing debate. At the heart of the debate is Section 43 of the Canadian Criminal Code. It allows parents, teachers, and guardians to use "force by way of correction toward a pupil or child . . .

if the force does not exceed what is reasonable under the circumstance." During the trial, Peterson's lawyer, Michael Menear, argued that the section protected parents who "honestly believe" they are teaching their children proper behavior and do not inflict injury in the process.

In his ruling, Justice John Menzies of the Ontario Court's Provincial Division said he was convinced the Petersons were "responsible, reasonable, and caring parents," and that the spanking of Rachel was not excessive. Menzies added that the testimony of Timperio – who acknowledged that she opposes physical discipline – "brings into sharp focus the different views in society on the subject of child discipline." Still, he added, "this is not a court of social justice, but of the law." 4

To many child experts and family workers, however, that law does not go far enough in protecting children. Dr. Elliott Barker, a psychiatrist who treats violent offenders, says that spanking can have "enormous costs" for both individuals and society. "To have the person you are most dependent on turn on you is a psychological blow you don't forget," says Barker. Children, he adds, will come to "believe that spanking is good, and they go on and spank their own kids." 5

After the trial, Paula Peterson declined to say whether she and her husband would continue to spank their children. "That's a decision my husband and I will make," she said. Both parents said that they had no hard feelings about the events of that day in the parking lot. 6

Adapted from *Maclean's*

A Comprehension Check

Put a check (✓) next to the item if the information is included in the reading. Then write the number of the paragraph where that information can be found.

_____ 1. the behavior of the child who was spanked (par. _____)

_____ 2. the name of the person who called the police (par. _____)

_____ 3. the names of experts who support spanking (par. _____)

_____ 4. the law the parent was accused of breaking (par. _____)

_____ 5. the laws against spanking in different parts of the world (par. _____)

_____ 6. a reason why parents shouldn't spank (par. _____)

_____ 7. the decision the Petersons made about spanking after the trial (par. _____)

B Vocabulary Study

Find the words in *italics* in the reading. Then match the words with their meanings in the box.

a. refused	b. causing disagreement	c. ending
d. a difficult experience	e. disrespectful	f. illegal hitting
g. criminals	h. freedom from criminal charges	

_____ 1. *insolent* (par. 1)

_____ 2. *ordeal* (par. 2)

_____ 3. *culminating* (par. 2)

_____ 4. *acquittal* (par. 2)

_____ 5. *assault* (par. 2)

_____ 6. *contentious* (par. 3)

_____ 7. *offenders* (par. 5)

_____ 8. *declined* (par. 6)

C Recognizing Point of View

> Sometimes a writer expresses a point of view, or an opinion. Other times, writers remain neutral and let readers come to their own conclusions. Recognizing whether or not the writer has expressed a point of view is an important part of reading critically.

Does the writer express a point of view about spanking or not? Check (✓) the most appropriate statement. Then compare your answer with a partner. Identify the parts of the reading that support your choice.

_____ 1. The writer supports spanking.

_____ 2. The writer opposes spanking.

_____ 3. The writer doesn't express an opinion.

D Relating Reading to Personal Experience

Discuss these questions with your classmates.

1. Do you think it is acceptable to spank a child? Why or why not?

2. Do you think Marlene Timperio was right or wrong to call the police? Why?

3. What is the most effective way for parents to punish two-year-olds? Six-year-olds? Nine-year-olds? Thirteen-year-olds? Seventeen-year-olds?

The Letter

Predicting

Look at the title, the picture, and the phrases from the reading in the box. What do you think happens in the story? Discuss your ideas with a partner.

"The neighborhood boy"	behave with dignity	"Forgive me."
this betrayal	put an end to this business	"Put this boy away now."
a mother's rage	"I've deceived you."	"Write your own letter."

Skimming

Skim the reading to check your prediction. Then read the whole text.

Her mother read the letter standing in the middle of the hut with one hand on her   1
forehead. While she read her lips moved rapidly, her eyes blinked severely and often.
Finished, she sat down on the edge of a chair, dangled the letter in her hand for a
moment, then sighed and took off her glasses. "Surely not," she said in Japanese.

She set the glasses in her lap wearily, placed the letter on top of them, and pressed   2
against her eyes with both palms.

"The neighborhood boy," she said aloud. "The one who taught her how to swim."   3

Now she stood with this letter in her hand – a letter a boy had sent to her daughter   4
about love. The depth of her deceit became vivid to Fujiko, and she felt in herself a
mother's rage at the weight of this betrayal.

She reminded herself to behave with dignity no matter what the circumstances, a   5
worthy lesson passed down from her grandmother. *Giri* was her grandmother's word for
it – it could not be precisely translated into English – and it meant doing what one had to
do quietly and with an entirely stoic demeanor.[1] Fujiko sat back and cultivated in herself

---

[1] *stoic demeanor:* appearance and behavior that shows no emotion

the spirit of quiet dignity that would be necessary in confronting Hatsue. She breathed deeply and shut her eyes.

6   Well, she told herself, she would have a talk with Hatsue when the girl came back from wandering aimlessly around the camp. She would put an end to this business.

7   At this moment Hatsue came through the door, her face reddened by the cold outside, and tugged the scarf from her head. When the door had shut, Fujiko reached behind her and handed Hatsue the letter. "Here," she spat. "Your mail. I don't know how you could have been so deceitful. I'll never understand it, Hatsue."

8   She had planned to discuss the matter right there and then, but she understood suddenly that the strength of her bitterness might prevent her from saying what she really meant. "You will not write again to this boy or accept his letters," she said sternly from the doorway.

9   The girl sat with the letter in her hand, tears gathering in her eyes. "I'm sorry," Hatsue said. "Forgive me, Mother. I've deceived you and I've always known it."

10   "Deceiving me," said Fujiko in Japanese, "is only half of it, daughter. You have deceived yourself, too."

11   Then Fujiko went out into the wind. She walked to the post office and told the clerk there to hold all mail for the Imada family. From now on, she herself would come for it. It should be handed to her only.

12   That afternoon she sat and wrote her own letter addressed to the boy's parents. She showed it to Hatsue when it was folded and ready to go into its envelope, then took it from her daughter's lap and ripped it neatly down the middle. "Write your own letter," she said in Japanese. "Tell him the truth about things. Put all of this in your history. Tell him the truth so you can move forward. Put this boy away now."

13   In the morning Fujiko took Hatsue's letter to the post office and paid the postage on it. She licked the envelope shut herself and, because the notion took hold of her suddenly – a kind of caprice and nothing more – she pressed the stamp on upside down before putting the letter in the mailbox.

Adapted from *Snow Falling On Cedars*

A Comprehension Check

Who does "she" refer to in the statements? Write *F* (Fujiko) or *H* (Hatsue).

_____ 1. She received a letter from a boy.

_____ 2. She read the letter the boy wrote.

_____ 3. She was angry.

_____ 4. She was apologetic.

_____ 5. She wrote a letter to the boy's family.

_____ 6. She wrote a letter to the boy.

_____ 7. She tore up the letter.

_____ 8. She mailed the letter.

B Vocabulary Study

Find the words in the reading that match these definitions.

1. held loosely   _____ (par. 1)

2. made a sound of sadness   _____ (par. 1)

3. parts of the hands   _____ (par. 2)

4. powerful and clear   _____ (par. 4)

5. valuable   _____ (par. 5)

6. telling someone why you are angry   _____ (par. 5)

7. not to deliver   _____ (par. 11)

8. tore quickly   _____ (par. 12)

C Making Inferences

> Sometimes the reader must infer, or figure out, what is true or what the writer did not explain or state directly in the text.

Answer the questions with a partner. Explain the reasons for your answers.

1. How old do you think Hatsue is?

2. What time of year do you think it is?

3. What do you think the boy wrote in his letter?

4. What do you think Hatsue wrote in her letter?

5. How would you describe Hatsue's character?

D Relating Reading to Personal Experience

Discuss these questions with your classmates.

1. Do you think Fujiko was right to forbid her daughter from communicating with the boy? Why or why not?

2. What would you have done if you had been in Hatsue's situation?

3. In your experience, do fathers and mothers differ in the way they punish their children? If so, how?

Schools Take the Fun Out of Suspensions

Thinking About the Topic

Look at the title of the reading. Then check (✓) the statements you agree with. Compare your answers with a partner.

_____ 1. Schools should punish students who misbehave.

_____ 2. Students who behave badly should be suspended.

_____ 3. Students who break rules should spend their suspension at home.

_____ 4. Students who behave badly should do extra work at school.

Skimming

Skim the reading to find out which statements Ventura County educators agree with. Then read the whole text.

1   Suspension just isn't what it used to be. Once, frustrated school officials could be sure that if they kicked a misbehaving student out of school, the student's angry and embarrassed parents would do the rest in terms of punishment.

2   But these days, too many parents are either working or they just don't care. In either case, these parents are not effective jailers. Therefore, for some students, suspension has become another holiday, all the sweeter because everyone else is in class.

3   Now, several principals in Ventura County, California, are having second thoughts about the whole concept of suspension. They are revamping discipline policies and endorsing a revolutionary approach to punishment. Instead of sending students home to the living room couch and daytime TV, they are keeping more troublemakers at school.

Students who break school rules are still suspended, but they are exiled on campus, where they catch up on homework, write personal goals, or clean up the school.

"It's not as much fun to be at school as it is to be at home," said Ventura County official 4
Miles Weiss. He believes that if you are a delinquent or you misbehave at school, you should suffer the consequences, not get a reward.

Administrators are also concerned about teens falling behind in their schoolwork. "We 5
want to keep students in school because that's our business," said principal Bob La Belle. "We don't want the students to fall further behind and penalize them unfairly for what may have happened in one class period." He said on-campus suspension prevents the "snowball effect," when a student who gets in trouble in one class is sent home for a few days and ends up behind in all six classes.

In several schools, teachers or campus supervisors watch over suspended students. 6
Some schools call their on-campus suspension classes "opportunity rooms." Educators say it's a good name, underscoring the idea that these are places where students have the opportunity to turn their lives around. School superintendent Chuck Weis says that bad behavior in school is an outward sign of an inner problem. "Suspension can give us an opportunity to work on that real underlying problem," he says.

Middle school students from Ventura are sent to a special "suspension school" held on 7
Fridays at Ventura College. They spend from 8 a.m. to 2 p.m. there, involved in activities aimed at controlling their anger, boosting their self-esteem, and improving their attitude toward school. For these students, the suspension doesn't show up on their school record.

At 8:15 a.m. on a recent Friday, teacher Peter Shedlosky asked the suspension school 8
students to introduce themselves: their names, grades, schools, and reason for suspension. A few kids' voices cracked as they took their turns reciting their transgressions: "I got kicked out of class. I pushed this guy. I beat up some kid. I got in a fight."

Ventura educators say having the suspension school on a college campus also 9
motivates the students to improve their behavior and grades. During the day, they take a tour of the college campus, look through the college catalog, and talk about careers.

At Westlake High School, students in the on-campus suspension program spend all 10
morning in various study hall classrooms. In the afternoon, they are handed trash bags and ordered to work. As they traverse the hillside and parking lot, they pick up coffee cups, soda cans, and fast-food bags. In this way, the suspension program serves both students and staff.

Adapted from *The Los Angeles Times*

A Comprehension Check

Check (✓) the main idea of the reading.

_____ 1. the reasons for suspension

_____ 2. one school's experience with suspension

_____ 3. suspension success stories

_____ 4. the problems caused by suspension

_____ 5. a new approach to suspension

_____ 6. middle school students' experience with suspension

B Vocabulary Study

Find the words in *italics* in the reading. Then match the words with their meanings.

_____ 1. *revamping* (par. 3)   a. the bad results of an action or event

_____ 2. *endorsing* (par. 3)   b. move across

_____ 3. *delinquent* (par. 4)   c. changing and improving

_____ 4. *consequences* (par. 4)   d. emphasizing

_____ 5. *underscoring* (par. 6)   e. a person who behaves very badly

_____ 6. *transgressions* (par. 8)   f. supporting

_____ 7. *traverse* (par. 10)   g. actions that break rules

C Recognizing Purpose

> Writers create texts for different purposes. For example, sometimes a writer wants to give information. Other times, the writer wants to persuade the reader to do something. Recognizing a writer's purpose will help you better understand what you read.

Check (✓) the writer's main purpose in the reading. Discuss the reasons for your answer with a partner.

_____ 1. to convince parents to support school officials' decisions

_____ 2. to describe the benefits of on-campus suspension programs

_____ 3. to inform educators of some modern punishment techniques

_____ 4. to give students the opportunity to express their opinions about suspension

D Relating Reading to Personal Experience

Discuss these questions with your classmates.

1. Who should punish misbehaving students – their parents or school officials? Why?

2. What kinds of misbehavior should students be punished for? What should teachers ignore?

3. Which on-campus suspension activities mentioned in the reading do you think would be the most effective? Why?

> Reread one of the unit readings and time yourself. Note your reading speed in the chart on page 124.

UNIT **7**  Memory

Look at the titles of the readings and their brief descriptions to preview this unit's content. Before you begin each reading, answer the questions about it.

Reading 1 ▶ **Can You Believe What You See?**

This newspaper article explains why our memories are not always as accurate as we think.

1. Have you ever witnessed a crime or an accident? If so, tell your classmates exactly what happened.

2. Can the police usually trust the report of an eyewitness at the scene of a crime or accident? Explain your answer.

3. Do you think you would be a good eyewitness? Why or why not?

Reading 2 ▶ **Man Weds the Wife He Forgot**

In this newspaper article, learn about how complete memory loss affected one man and those around him.

1. What are some causes of memory loss?

2. Were there people or events in your past that you don't remember clearly now? If so, give examples.

3. What can be done to help someone who has lost his or her memory?

Reading 3 ▶ **Repeat After Me: Memory Takes Practice**

Why do we forget things? This newspaper article provides some answers and suggests ways to improve memory.

1. What do you do to help you remember things?

2. Which of your classes require you to remember the most information? Which ones require the least memorization?

3. How does a good memory help students in school?

Can You Believe What You See?

Thinking About the Topic

Look at the title of the reading. Then check (✓) the statements you think are true. Compare your answers with a partner.

_____ 1. Witnesses of a crime sometimes change their stories when they hear new information.

_____ 2. Adults can be convinced that, as children, they experienced events that never happened.

_____ 3. Witnesses' memories are affected by the amount of time they observe something.

_____ 4. It doesn't matter how long after a crime an eyewitness is interviewed.

Skimming

Skim the reading to check your answers. Then read the whole text.

1   A crime has been committed. The police are sure they have the right guy in custody. After all, they have an eyewitness. But should they be so sure? "No," claim psychologists who have studied eyewitness testimony.

2   Daniel Wright, a psychologist at Sussex University, has found that when witnesses are given misleading information after an incident, some will adapt their memories to accommodate this new information. In one experiment, 40 students looked at a series of pictures showing the story of two men meeting at a pool hall and of a woman later stealing one man's wallet. Each student studied the pictures on his or her own.

3   Without any of the volunteers knowing, half of the group had slightly different information from the other half. Twenty students saw a picture showing the woman loitering outside the pool hall on her own before the crime. The other half saw a picture of her loitering with an accomplice.

When questioned afterward, individually, about whether the woman had an accomplice, 39 of the 40 students got it right. Then the students were paired off so that, in each pair, only one had seen the picture featuring the accomplice and one had viewed the picture without the accomplice.   4

Each pair was asked to discuss what they knew, and to answer the question jointly: Did the woman have an accomplice?   5

Since the members of each pair had seen different scenarios, none of them should have reached agreement. In fact, 15 pairs did reach an agreement. (Eight pairs reported no accomplice, while seven reported the opposite.) In other words, 15 witnesses were swayed by what their partner had told them.   6

One reason why our memories change is that, when given information, we use it to fill visual gaps. Wright explains: "Imagine a police officer saying, 'I want to ask you about the collision between the red car and green car. Was there a yield sign at the intersection?' If you can't remember the colors, you may use this information to fill the gaps, and you may later remember the cars being red and green."   7

False memories can even be planted from scratch. Give people a selection of childhood memories, three of which are true and one is false (the experimenters collaborate with parents), and many subjects will come to believe, quite strongly, that all were genuine experiences. "You can convince adult volunteers that they were lost in a shopping mall as a child even though parents confirm that such an event never took place," he says.   8

So how can the police get the best out of eyewitnesses? Wright says that the best cases are where observers have been able to watch a culprit for a while rather than seeing them for a fleeting moment. All interviews should be conducted as soon as possible, with witnesses freely recalling what happened and not subjected to leading questions.   9

"If you give memory too much of a helping hand, memories will appear, whether they are true or not," Wright says.   10

Adapted from *The Times (London)*

A Comprehension Check

Work with a partner. Complete the sentences with information about Dr. Wright's experiment.

1. Dr. Wright, like other psychologists, has studied _____.

2. In the experiment, 40 students looked at _____.

3. Twenty students saw the woman with someone; 20 saw the woman _____.

4. When questioned individually about the pictures, _____ students were able to accurately report the number of people in their picture.

5. When students discussed the answers in pairs, _____ students reported that there was someone with the woman, even though they had seen a picture of the woman alone.

6. Dr. Wright showed that when you give witnesses misleading information, some will

_____.

B Vocabulary Study

Find the words in *italics* in the reading. Then match the words with their meanings.

_____ 1. *loitering* (par. 3)   a. real

_____ 2. *accomplice* (par. 3)   b. together

_____ 3. *jointly* (par. 5)   c. things that are missing

_____ 4. *swayed* (par. 6)   d. staying in a public place with no reason to be there

_____ 5. *gaps* (par. 7)   e. remembering

_____ 6. *genuine* (par. 8)   f. persuaded someone to believe something

_____ 7. *recalling* (par. 9)   g. a person who helps to commit a crime

C Identifying Main Ideas and Supporting Details

> Identifying the main ideas and supporting details in a text is an important strategy that will help your reading comprehension. It's a good idea to find the main ideas first. Then look for the supporting details that explain the main ideas more fully.

Identify which sentence in each pair is the main idea and which is the supporting detail. Write *MI* (main idea) or *SD* (supporting detail).

1. _____ a. Some psychologists say that witnesses adapt their memories to include new information.
   _____ b. Daniel Wright has studied eyewitness testimony.

2. _____ a. If a police officer mentions red and green cars, you may remember them.
   _____ b. We use new information to fill visual gaps.

3. _____ a. You can convince adults of childhood events that never occurred.
   _____ b. False memories can be created from scratch.

4. _____ a. There are ways to get good information from eyewitnesses.
   _____ b. Talk to eyewitnesses as soon as possible.

D Relating Reading to Personal Experience

Discuss these questions with your classmates.

1. What questions do the police usually ask an eyewitness of a crime or accident?

2. Do you remember things that happened to you as a child? Do you think other members of your family would agree with your memory of the events?

3. What do you remember about the first time this class met? Do your classmates agree?

Man Weds the Wife He Forgot

Predicting

Look at the title of the reading. Then check (✓) the information you think you will find in the text. Compare your answers with a partner.

_____ 1. After his first wife's death, a man married his childhood sweetheart.

_____ 2. A man married a woman twice because he couldn't remember the first wedding.

_____ 3. A man married a second woman because he didn't remember that he was married.

_____ 4. A man missed his wedding because he forgot he was getting married.

_____ 5. A man had difficulty remembering things all of his life.

_____ 6. A man lost his memory in a car accident.

Skimming

Skim the reading to check your prediction. Then read the whole text.

To Ken Howell, four decades of his life are a closed book. 1

A brain tumor caused such a catastrophic memory loss that he was left believing he 2 was still a teenager in the 1950s. He thought modern cars looked like space ships, had never heard of the Kennedy assassination or The Beatles, and was shocked to learn that Elvis Presley was dead.

Worst of all, he did not even know that 3 he was married or that he was the father of three grown children. With infinite care and patience, however, his wife Christine introduced 56-year-old Mr. Howell to life in the twenty-first century, and he fell in love with her all over again.

Mrs. Howell said, "We 4 have both had good careers, we have

worked hard, had three beautiful children and a lovely home. The children had all left home, and we were looking forward to a wonderful future together when Ken suddenly fell ill.

5   "He had a bad cold for a while and severe headaches. Eventually things got so bad that he was sent to the hospital, he slipped into a coma, and was diagnosed as having cancer of the brain."

6   Mrs. Howell stayed at his bedside for three months and, miraculously, he recovered. "But when he came out of the coma, he did not know who I was," she said. "It was the same with the children; they were strangers to him. When I took him home, he was reluctant to come with me, but he did. When I told him I was his wife, he said, 'You can't be, you're too old.'

7   "Worst of all was not remembering me and the children because we had been so close. At first he thought I was nursing him, and he had no idea who the children were. He would just send them away when they came to visit.

8   "But softly, softly through videos and photographs, he has clawed back some of his past, although he does find it all very upsetting, as you can imagine. One day I managed to get him to watch the video of Karen's wedding. He gave her away and made speeches at all of his children's weddings. Tears came running down his face. He said, 'I want to get married again.' He said he had to do it so he could have a memory of his marriage. It was so romantic."

9   Mr. Howell said, "It has been a very hard three years, especially for Christine and the children. I have found it very hard not remembering things. I cannot remember meeting Christine or getting married or having children – all those wonderful moments in a man's life.

10   "I had to watch a video of man walking on the moon because I just refused to believe Christine when she told me it had happened. The cars people drive these days, the cost of everything, the way houses are, the way people dress and speak, music, modern technology – it's all a bit strange to a man stuck in the late '50s.

11   "I got to thinking that everything I was being told must be true, and I have fallen in love with Christine all over again. I cried with joy when she said she would marry me again."

Adapted from *The Sunday Telegraph*

A Comprehension Check

Answer these questions with a partner.

1. What caused Ken's memory loss?

2. What important people in his life could he not remember?

3. How did Christine try to help Ken remember things?

4. What important events in his life could he not remember?

5. When Ken got better, what things surprised him about modern life?

B Vocabulary Study

Find the words and phrases in *italics* in the reading. Then circle the letters of the correct meanings.

1. *a closed book* (par. 1)
   a. something you can't read
   b. something you know nothing about
   c. something very interesting
   d. someone's life story

2. *slipped into a coma* (par. 5)
   a. fell down
   b. spent time in the hospital
   c. had an operation
   d. became unconscious

3. *recovered* (par. 6)
   a. put covers on again
   b. got help in a hospital
   c. became well after an illness
   d. got sick again

4. *reluctant* (par. 6)
   a. not willing
   b. not able
   c. excited
   d. worried

5. *clawed back* (par. 8)
   a. complained
   b. obtained, or got, something again
   c. forgot several times
   d. thought about

6. *gave her away* (par. 8)
   a. told her secret
   b. gave her a gift
   c. revealed her feelings
   d. presented the bride to the groom

C Summarizing

> When you summarize a text, you include only the most important information. A summary does not include details or examples. Summarizing is a strategy that can help you check your understanding of a text.

Cross out the sentences that don't belong in the summary.

A man lost his memory because of an illness. His hospital stay was three months long. When he recovered, he thought he was a teenager again, and he could not remember his wife or his children. His wife's name was Christine. Looking at photographs helped him recover some of his memories. He looked at pictures of his daughter's wedding. He asked his wife to marry him again so that he could have a memory of his own wedding.

D Relating Reading to Personal Experience

Discuss these questions with your classmates.

1. What memorable world events have happened during your life so far?

2. What are some personal memories that you wouldn't want to forget?

3. What things do you have that will help you remember the past when you get older?

Repeat After Me: Memory Takes Practice

Thinking About What You Know

What do you know about memory? Mark each statement *T* (true) or *F* (false). Compare your answers with a partner.

_____ 1. Only the elderly worry about memory loss.

_____ 2. Even good students forget things.

_____ 3. Students normally have memory lapses over long school vacations.

_____ 4. The amount of time students study doesn't affect their memory of a subject.

_____ 5. Learning to remember information better will make you smarter.

Skimming

Skim the reading to check your answers. Then read the whole text.

1   Meghan Pierce is a high school senior whose excellent memory has helped her achieve top grades. But asked which of last year's lessons she is forgetting this summer, she joked, "Everything."

2   It's not the summer sun causing the lapses. Pierce says she's having the most trouble remembering Spanish and history facts, and brain experts say the problem is infrequency of use. Memory lapses, once chiefly the worry of the elderly, have emerged as a source of anxiety among folks of all ages in this era of information overload.

3   "My mom will tell me to do a chore, and I'll walk upstairs to get the vacuum cleaner, and I'll have to walk back downstairs to ask her what I was supposed to do," said Pierce. "There are just so many things on our minds."

4   Researchers say memory can indeed be improved, and the keys to achieving it are simpler than you might think – lots of practice and better organization. Not to mention focus, something that was reinforced for renowned cellist Yo-Yo Ma after he left his $2.5 million, 266-year-old cello in a New York taxi. (It was recovered.)

Misplace keys? Keep them in the same place every day. Forget names? Use word 5
associations. Fearful of forgetting a special occasion? Tell your brain the date is important,
and repeat it to yourself again and again.

That doesn't mean it is easy to improve memory; studies by manufacturers of herbs 6
that claim to do so have been challenged by many leading scientists. It also doesn't mean
that learning how to retain certain information makes someone inherently smarter.

New research is showing that memories can be diminished by stress and even by 7
physical trauma. Young soccer players who take a lot of headshots report some mild
memory problems.

Besides, experts say, forgetting some things is normal. "We function so well as human 8
beings because in fact we forget things at a very efficient rate," said neuroscientist James
L. Olds. "If we flawlessly remember everything about every aspect of every day, we would
have tremendous difficulty given the fact that our brains are limited . . . Forgetting is as
important biologically as memory."

And forgetting long division over the summer doesn't count because the information 9
isn't really "lost." The foundation has probably been retained in the brain, and it can be
easily retrieved with review in the fall, experts said.

What students generally lose over the summer are isolated facts not associated with 10
images and not embedded in a larger framework, said Ira B. Black, at the Robert Wood
Johnson Medical School in New Jersey. "In a sense, then, you have to care to remember,"
he said.

It is also easier to forget information that is new and different, said psychology 11
professor Alan S. Brown. "If you have been studying English grammar all year, it
is less likely to be forgotten than the Spanish which you first started taking in the
spring semester."

High school student Lyndsey Wilson agreed. "All the stuff they teach in one day I 12
forget. We learned World War II over three weeks, and I remember that."

Adapted from *The Washington Post*

A Comprehension Check

Circle the letter of the correct answer based on what the experts say.

1. Students have trouble remembering
   things over summer vacation because
   they _____.
   a. get too much sun
   b. have too much on their minds
   c. don't use what they learned

2. To improve your memory, you do *not*
   need to _____.
   a. study facts
   b. practice
   c. be organized

3. Forgetting is _____.
   a. not caused by stress or injury
   b. normal
   c. a sign of a lack of intelligence

4. Over the summer, it's easier for students
   to remember information that is _____.
   a. new and different
   b. taught in one day
   c. associated with images

B Vocabulary Study

Find the words and phrases in the reading that match these definitions. The number of blanks represents the number of words in the answer.

1. too much of something   _____ (par. 2)

2. thinking about a lot   _____ _____ _____ (par. 3)

3. the most important ways or methods   _____ (par. 4)

4. provided proof   _____ (par. 4)

5. famous   _____ (par. 4)

6. reduced in amount, size, or strength   _____ (par. 7)

7. without mistakes   _____ (par. 8)

8. gotten back; remembered   _____ (par. 9)

C Understanding Pronoun Reference

> Writers use different kinds of pronouns to refer to information that is stated earlier in a text. Some common pronouns are *it*, *her*, and *that*. Understanding pronoun reference is very important for reading comprehension.

What do these words refer to?

1. *her* (par. 1, line 1)   _____

2. *it* (par. 4, line 1)   _____

3. *It* (par. 4, line 4)   _____

4. *it* (par. 5, line 3)   _____

5. *it* (par. 9, line 2)   _____

6. *that* (par. 12, line 2)   _____

D Relating Reading to Personal Experience

Discuss these questions with your classmates.

> Reread one of the unit readings and time yourself. Note your reading speed in the chart on page 124.

1. What are (or were) the easiest subjects for you to remember in school? Why do you think this is true?

2. What information in the reading do you agree with? Is there any information that you disagree with? If so, explain why.

3. Have you studied some information recently that you have already forgotten? If so, how long did you study it?

UNIT 8 Personality

Look at the titles of the readings and their brief descriptions to preview this unit's content. Before you begin each reading, answer the questions about it.

Reading 1

What Do Our Possessions Say About Us?

This newspaper article describes the results of a study linking possessions to personality.

1. What do a person's possessions reveal about his or her personality?

2. Have you ever looked through someone's music collection or bookshelves?

3. What personality traits do you like?

Reading 2

Temperament and Personality

In this book excerpt, you learn how people's temperament and personality affect their behavior.

1. Do you have a predisposition, or tendency, to be sociable or shy? Explain your answer.

2. Do you think people's normal way of behaving changes as they get older? If so, how?

3. Why do you think people often react differently to the same situation?

Reading 3

Mind Your P's and Q's

How much can you tell about people from their handwriting? This magazine article provides some answers.

1. What are some characteristics of your handwriting?

2. Do you know anyone who has unusual handwriting? If so, describe it.

3. Does your handwriting change when you write in a different language? If so, how?

What Do Our Possessions Say About Us?

Thinking About the Topic

How would you describe the personality of someone who keeps the items listed below in his or her room? For example, could the person be *ambitious*, *unconventional*, *creative*, *scatterbrained*, or *agreeable*? Discuss your ideas with a partner.

- A piranha
- A poster showing teamwork
- A poster of a hip rock star
- An overflowing in-tray
- A basket of candy

Scanning

Scan the reading and circle the listed items. Find out what the writer says about people who have these things in their rooms. Then read the whole text.

1   On top of my computer sits a desiccated piranha with a mouthful of razor-sharp teeth. Why is that fish there? To remind me of that wonderful trip to Venezuela? To signal I'm not to be messed with? Maybe it's there because I'm a creative, unconventional individual who refuses to be stifled by the corporate office culture. Or maybe it's because that's what I want people to think.

2   If one little dried-out fish can potentially carry that much information, just think how much could be gleaned from a roomful of possessions. And we are constantly trying to glean. Who hasn't nosed through a bookshelf in someone's home to get some idea of their host's personality? "It's a basic human need to want to know what people are like, for all kinds of reasons: Can we trust them? Are they a potential mate?" says Samuel Gosling, assistant professor of psychology. "So, when we're in places where information is rich, we make use of it."

3   Not everything we deduce will be accurate, of course. People may display misleading messages. Someone who's ruthlessly ambitious might adorn his or her office with inspirational posters applauding teamwork. A conservative college kid may flaunt posters of hip rock stars to appear cool.

What's more, observers may guess erroneously from what they see. The fact that I have a two-foot-high in-tray doesn't mean I'm scatterbrained and undependable. And who knows what my co-worker with the welcoming basket of candy and smiley-face pencil is thinking? 4

To find out what people deduce from someone's "social environment" – and whether those deductions are accurate – Gosling enrolled 83 students and 94 office workers in a study. All agreed to have their bedrooms (in the students' case) or offices assessed by observers. 5

Participants were told not to alter anything. And even if they did rush around picking up sweaty socks, "there's a big difference between a tidied room and one that's deeply tidy," Gosling says. "There's only so much you can do in a short time to alphabetize the books, color-code the stationery, sharpen all your pencils and line them up – things that deeply tidy people do." 6

Each assessor then scored the occupant on a scale of one to seven for five broad personality traits: 7

* openness to new experiences
* agreeableness
* extroversion
* emotional stability (how calm, relaxed, and self-assured someone is)
* conscientiousness or dependability (whether someone shows up for meetings and pays parking tickets on time)

To test the results, Gosling and colleagues compared raters' assessments to ones done by occupants and friends. Raters gleaned a lot in just a few minutes, Gosling says. They weren't great at assessing agreeableness and extroversion, but they were surprisingly adept at scoring someone's dependability and openness to new experiences. 8

Gosling notes that some employers prohibit the personalization of office spaces. Might this damage morale? "The fact that wherever I go I see these expressions of individuality leaking out makes me think it probably isn't a good thing to do." He plans to explore this by having pairs of students decorate each other's living quarters. 9

"What, for instance, would happen if I made you trade your piranha for an angel?" he says. "You'd probably find it very distressing." As, very likely, would anyone who befriended me based on that angel. 10

Adapted from *The Los Angeles Times*

A Comprehension Check

Circle the letter of the correct answer.

1. What is the author's main point?
   a. People's possessions reflect their personalities completely.
   b. People's possessions do not reflect their personalities at all.
   c. People's possessions usually reflect their personalities, but some of their things may lead others to the wrong conclusions.

2. The author supports the main point by _____.
   a. describing a research study   b. interviewing people   c. giving her own opinions

3. Does Gosling think it's bad for employees to decorate their offices?
   a. yes   b. no   c. sometimes

B Vocabulary Study

Match the words from the reading that are similar in meaning.

_____ 1. *desiccated* (par. 1)   a. *display* (par. 3)

_____ 2. *gleaned* (par. 2 & 8)   b. *dried-out* (par. 2)

_____ 3. *adorn* (par. 3)   c. *home* (par. 2)

_____ 4. *flaunt* (par. 3)   d. *find out* (par. 5)

_____ 5. *assessed* (par. 5 & 8)   e. *scored* (par. 7 & 8)

_____ 6. *living quarters* (par. 9)   f. *decorate* (par. 9)

C Making Inferences

Sometimes the reader must infer, or figure out, what the writer did not explain or state directly in the text.

Mark each statement *I* (inference) or *F* (fact stated in the reading).

_I_ 1. The writer of the text once took a trip to Venezuela.

_____ 2. Ambitious people are not usually interested in teamwork.

_____ 3. Gosling used students and office workers in his study.

_____ 4. Participants were not supposed to change the appearance of their rooms.

_____ 5. The assessors were better at scoring some personality traits than others.

_____ 6. The assessors quickly made decisions about personality traits.

_____ 7. People should be allowed to display personal possessions at work.

_____ 8. If people see an angel in somebody's office, they might think the person is nice.

D Relating Reading to Personal Experience

Discuss these questions with your classmates.

1. What kinds of possessions do you have? What do you think they say about you?

2. How do you decorate your room or office? What do you think this conveys to others?

3. Do you judge people based on their possessions? Why or why not?

Temperament and Personality

Previewing Vocabulary

The words in the box are from the reading. Discuss the meanings of the words with a partner. Look up any new words in a dictionary. Then tell your partner which words describe you.

expressive	generous	inhibited	joyous
outgoing	restless	sullen	withdrawn

Scanning

Scan the reading. Find and circle the words from the box. Then read the whole text.

Why do I need everything to be completely shipshape? Why am I always getting into battles with my boss and my children? Why is my sister so restless while I'm quite happy to sit home and read? What's wrong with me, or is there something wrong with her? Why am I always so happy while my wife is often sad, even when we're both on vacation? My brother is a much harder worker than I am; how can I match him? Most of us ask ourselves these questions at least occasionally; others concentrate on them almost constantly and spend lots of time and money to come up with answers.

Parents know that their children are born with very definite dispositions. "He was always a quiet little boy," they'll say, or "She was always climbing trees and looking for excitement." We all have an inherent temperament — to be sociable and outgoing or shy and withdrawn.

1

2

3   Modern psychologists use the word *temperament* to refer to a person's predisposition to behave in a certain way. Temperament refers to the style rather than to the content of behavior. We might say that it is the "how" of behavior, not the "what." It concerns whether one generally seeks excitement or sits alone, whether one is usually highly expressive or inhibited, joyous or sullen.

4   Personality, on the other hand, is the full-blown complex set of traits that distinguish an individual. We would need to list hundreds of particulars in order to describe a person we know well: slow to anger, tough when provoked, generally calm, reads the sports pages, generous, athletic.

5   Each of us forms our own theories of individuality. We use these ideas not only to characterize other people ("Joe is an honest person.") but also to predict ("Morgan is generous, so I'll ask her if I can borrow a ten."). Belief in the importance of personality traits rests on the assumption that knowing a person's characteristics will tell us something about how that individual will behave. Trying to predict how anyone will act, however, is a bit like trying to predict the weather in some random month from now in a random place at a random time.

6   We tend to see how a person behaves and then attribute that behavior to a basic personality trait. Most of us assume that these traits consistently influence others' behavior. We think that someone who is honest never lies to friends, does not cheat, and doesn't steal. But we are often wrong. Some psychologists question whether people really are consistent enough across situations to make knowledge of personality useful in predicting behavior. This very complexity, however, is probably what keeps most of us interested in each other, as we puzzle over how to piece together an accurate picture of another person.

Adapted from *Roots of the Self*

A Comprehension Check

Every paragraph in the reading has one main idea. Write the correct paragraph number for each main idea.

_____ a. This paragraph discusses individuality.

_____ b. This paragraph shows how parents describe their children.

_____ c. This paragraph questions the usefulness of personality in predicting behavior.

_____ d. This paragraph illustrates differences between people.

_____ e. This paragraph defines personality.

_____ f. This paragraph defines temperament.

B Vocabulary Study

Find the words in *italics* in the reading. Then match the words with their meanings in the box.

a. details	b. think of something as the result	c. existing at birth
d. neat	e. something that is accepted as true	f. chosen by chance

_____ 1. *shipshape* (par. 1)

_____ 2. *inherent* (par. 2)

_____ 3. *particulars* (par. 4)

_____ 4. *assumption* (par. 5)

_____ 5. *random* (par. 5)

_____ 6. *attribute to* (par. 6)

C Recognizing Contrast in a Text

Sometimes writers contrast, or show the difference between, ideas in a text. They often use words or phrases such as *but* and *on the other hand* to signal the contrast.

Read these two passages from the reading. In each passage, circle the words and phrases that signal contrast. Then draw an arrow between the ideas being contrasted.

1. Why do I need everything to be completely shipshape? Why am I always getting into battles with my boss and children? Why is my sister so restless while I'm quite happy to sit home and read? What's wrong with me, or is there something wrong with her? Why am I always so happy while my wife is so often sad, even when we're both on vacation?

2. Modern psychologists use the word *temperament* to refer to a person's predisposition to behave in a certain way. Temperament refers to the style rather than to the content of behavior. We might say that it is the "how" of behavior, not the "what." It concerns whether one generally seeks excitement or sits alone, whether one is usually highly expressive or inhibited, joyous or sullen.

   Personality, on the other hand, is the full-blown complex set of traits that distinguish an individual. We would need to list hundreds of particulars in order to describe a person we know well.

D Relating Reading to Personal Experience

Discuss these questions with your classmates.

1. Compare your temperament to that of someone in your family.

2. Which personality traits in other people do you find annoying?

3. How would you describe your best friend's personality?

Mind Your P's and Q's

Thinking About What You Know

Work with a partner. Look at the handwriting samples. What can you tell about each writer's personality? Write two characteristics for each sample.

1. _____ _____

2. _____ _____

3. _____ _____

Skimming

Skim the reading and underline the words and phrases that describe the personalities of the writers of these samples. Then read the whole text.

1   As you're gathering love letters from your admirers on Valentine's Day, wouldn't it be nice to know if that special sweetie is Mr. or Ms. Right? While it's not scientific, graphology – also called handwriting analysis – can provide useful clues about your amour's personality. "In this country, handwriting analysis is considered akin to astrology – something not taken very seriously – but it probably tells us more about a human being than any psychological test," says Ted Widmer, director of the International School of Handwriting Sciences. He provides basic hints for deciphering that love note.

2   Ideally, handwriting analysis should be performed on an unlined page of original writing, not a photocopy or fax. When studying a sample, the first characteristic a graphologist considers is the writer's use of space: "There are universal concepts people in all societies and cultures have regarding the use of space," notes Widmer.

Left and right margins

3   The right symbolizes the future and the left represents the past – even in cultures that use the Arabic or Hebrew alphabets and whose writing moves from right to left. In graphology, leaving a narrow right margin suggests a risk-taking person who is unafraid

of the future, whereas leaving a narrow left margin implies someone very tied to the past, even fearful of moving on.

Writing that moves uphill or downhill

"The symbolism of this is revealed in everyday language," says Widmer. "If you're feeling good, you're 'up,' and if you're feeling bad, you're 'down.' Handwriting reflects this." Thus, writing that tends to slope upward from left to right indicates an optimistic attitude, whereas handwriting drifting downward is often a sign of tiredness, sadness, or possibly depression.

4

Space between words and lines

This represents the distance the writer places between himself – or herself – and others. Thus, people who leave relatively little space between words require others' company – "They're needier, and possibly insecure," notes Widmer – while those who leave more space may be hard to get close to. Similarly, people who leave little space between lines need to get involved: "They tend to be big 'joiners,' and may get bogged down in the details of a situation," says Widmer. By contrast, writers who leave more space between lines are usually more independent and better at grasping the "big picture."

5

Besides space, graphologists also consider the zones writing is divided into: the upper (tall letters), middle (round letters), and lower (letters that extend downward). The balance among these three is very revealing. Here's what to look for:

6

The upper zone symbolizes one's mental and spiritual life; thus, someone whose handwriting features very tall letters tends to be an intellectual, "thinking" type. The middle zone, meanwhile, represents the everyday and how the person sees him- or herself in relation to others. "People with a very large middle zone – rounded letters with little difference in height – are relatively self-centered and immature," says Widmer. "You often see this trait in teenagers' handwriting." Finally, the lower zone stands for one's physical side; athletes and other physical types often write with pronounced lower zones.

7

Widmer cautions that while these are generally accepted concepts of graphology, no single characteristic in writing is significant by itself. "It's not correct to say that crossing your *T* a certain way means something," he notes. "You have to look at handwriting in context."

8

Adapted from Successful Meetings

A Comprehension Check

Look at the handwriting samples on the opposite page. Then answer the questions. Write *1, 2,* or *3.*

_____ a. Who probably looks forward to the future?

_____ b. Who probably has few close friends?

_____ c. Who probably doesn't like to spend time alone?

_____ d. Who is probably a member of many organizations?

_____ e. Who probably doesn't worry about details?

_____ f. Who probably does silly things for his or her age?

B Vocabulary Study

Find the words or phrases in the reading that match these definitions. The number of blanks represents the number of words in the answer.

1. discovering the meaning of something complicated   _____ (par. 1)

2. connected to   _____ _____ (par. 3)

3. wanting more from others   _____ (par. 5)

4. unable to make progress   _____ _____ _____ (par. 5)

5. understanding   _____ (par. 5)

6. making something known   _____ (par. 6)

7. very noticeable   _____ (par. 7)

C Identifying Supporting Details

> Sometimes writers use examples as supporting details. If you can identify examples in a text, you will have a clearer understanding of the writer's ideas.

Look back at the reading and find examples to support these general statements.

1. The right margin symbolizes the future, and the left margin symbolizes the past.

   A narrow right margin: _a risk-taking person who is unafraid of the future_

   A narrow left margin: _____

2. If you're feeling good, you're "up," and if you're feeling bad, you're "down."

   Upward writing: _____

   Downward writing: _____

3. The distance between words represents the distance the writer places between himself – or herself – and others.

   Little space between words/lines: _____

   More space between words/lines: _____

D Relating Reading to Personal Experience

Discuss these questions with your classmates.

1. Would you pay for a professional handwriting analysis? Why or why not?

2. Do you think employers should use graphology to make hiring decisions? Explain your answer.

3. Look at something you've written recently. According to the reading, what does your handwriting say about your personality? Do you agree? Why or why not?

> Reread one of the unit readings and time yourself. Note your reading speed in the chart on page 124.

UNIT 9 Fashion

Look at the titles of the readings and their brief descriptions to preview this unit's content. Before you begin each reading, answer the questions about it.

Reading 1

Smart Clothes

How will technology influence the clothes we wear? This Internet article provides insights into the future role of hi-tech textiles.

1. Smart clothing is clothing with tiny motors and transmitters that transport electrical current. What functions do you think smart clothing could have?

2. How could smart clothing be useful in health-related matters?

3. If you were a superhero like Spiderman or Wonder Woman, what special powers would you like to have? How could smart clothing help you?

Reading 2

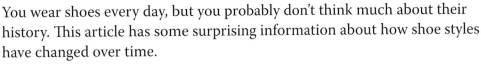

Shoes

You wear shoes every day, but you probably don't think much about their history. This article has some surprising information about how shoe styles have changed over time.

1. What kind of footwear do you wear? For example, how often do you wear each of these: *boots, casual shoes, dress shoes, sandals, slippers, sneakers*?

2. When you buy shoes, how important is comfort? What about cost and style? Is one factor more important than the others?

3. What is your favorite type of shoe? Why?

Reading 3

Style, Not Fashion

The writer of this article says that style is a unique blend of spirit (our inner selves) and substance (the things we choose to wear). Is fashion the same as style?

1. How interested are you in fashion? For example, do you look at fashion magazines? Do you buy things that are in fashion? Why or why not?

2. How would you describe your style? Do you try to look distinctive, or do you prefer to look like most other people?

3. Do you vary your style according to the situation – for example, school, work, parties? In what ways does your style vary?

Smart Clothes

1

2

3

Predicting

Look at the pictures and match the article of clothing to what you think it might be able to do.

_____ 1. glove   a. act as a cell phone

_____ 2. tank top   b. alert the wearer to an approaching danger

_____ 3. vest   c. monitor a person's heart rate

Skimming

Skim the first paragraph to see if you matched the items correctly. Then read the whole text.

1   A glove that works as a cell phone, a vest that senses danger, and a tank top that measures heart rate. It seems that the hi-tech textiles by Swedish School of Textiles researcher Lena Berglin could turn anyone into a superhero.

2   A few years ago, Lena Berglin started her new research project by dismantling her earlier invention, the cell phone glove. By putting the parts together with another interactive product, a whole new textile product was created: the electrocardiogram (ECG) tank top. It has sensors that measure your heart rate and breathing frequency while you're out jogging, for example.

3   "I wanted to do something that gave a positive health effect and made life easier," Berglin says. Her idea is not to create superheroes, though, but to help normal people with health problems. "Someone who has had a heart attack and is worried about getting back into exercising may find it easier with a tank top like this."

In cooperation with the Swedish National Institute for Working Life (now closed) and the Centre for Biomedical Engineering and Physics at Umeå University, Berglin has developed a whole range of garments for monitoring health. In addition to the tank top, it also includes a cardigan and a belt. They all measure heart rate, breathing rate, and muscular activity. **4**

The cardigan was developed because it is very easy to wear on top of other clothes. The cuffs of this garment measure the body functions of the wearer, and a box with the battery and the transmitter can be stored in the cardigan pocket. **5**

For the ECG tank top, the future looks bright. "The U.S. market is very interested," Berglin says. "The Americans want the technology and have customers that are used to paying for health care." **6**

Working with the Swedish Army, she has also developed a vest. The vest has tiny motors embedded in silicon and, through radar communication, wearers can be alerted to danger before their eyes or ears have even managed to record it. Did you know that your skin reacts faster than your eyes and ears? **7**

The unifying theme of Berglin's projects is electroactive textiles. Using metals, she creates surfaces on the textiles that transmit a current. The textiles she has developed for monitoring breathing can, for example, be used to help children born prematurely. "My research has always been very applicable," Berglin says. "I combine technology and design." **8**

The smart textile concept is used for protective clothing design, such as health care uniforms and sportswear, and also in interior decorating, construction, the car industry, and the manufacture of biomedical implants. **9**

"Smart textiles have attracted a lot of attention lately, and you might even say they are at their peak right now," Berglin says. "That's why it's important to live up to the demands. We still have a few problems that we need to find solutions to." **10**

So, to all you superheroes out there: Don't worry, our super-researchers will keep inventing super-smart textiles to help you make the world a better place. **11**

Adapted from http://www.sweden.se/eng/Home/Education/Research/
Reading/Swedish-hi-tech-clothing--the-perfect-superhero-outfit/

A Comprehension Check

Work with a partner and answer the following questions.

1. Why has Lena Berglin developed smart clothing? (par. 3)

2. What do Berglin's cardigan, tank top, and belt all do? (par. 4)

3. What is the difference between the cardigan and the tank top? (par. 5)

4. Who is interested in buying Berglin's tank top and vest? (par. 6)

5. Why are they interested in them? (par. 6)

6. What is the one thing that all Berglin's projects have in common? (par. 8)

7. Besides clothing, what other uses are there for smart textiles? (par. 9)

B Vocabulary Study

Find the words in *italics* in the reading. Then circle the letters of the correct meanings.

_____ 1. *dismantling* (par. 2)
   a. making   b. studying   c. taking apart

_____ 2. *garments* (pars. 4 & 5)
   a. articles of clothing   b. hi-tech devices   c. medical equipment

_____ 3. *monitoring* (pars. 4 & 8)
   a. carefully watching   b. helpfully making   c. secretly listening

_____ 4. *bright* (par. 6)
   a. full of light   b. intelligent   c. encouraging

_____ 5. *peak* (par. 10)
   a. cheapest price   b. highest point   c. most stylish

_____ 6. *live up to* (par. 10)
   a. be as good as expected   b. find solutions   c. give people homes

C Understanding Pronoun Reference

> Writers use different kinds of pronouns to refer to information that is stated earlier in a text. Two common pronouns are *it* and *they*. Understanding pronoun reference is very important for reading comprehension.

What do these words refer to?

1. *It* (par. 2, line 4) _____

2. *it* (par. 3, line 4) _____

3. *it* (par. 4, line 4) _____

4. *They* (par. 4, line 5) _____

5. *it* (par. 7, line 3) _____

6. *they* (par. 10, line 2) _____

D Relating Reading to Personal Experience

Discuss these questions with your classmates.

1. Which of the smart clothing ideas mentioned in the article sounds especially useful to you? Why?

2. If there was a piece of smart clothing that you wanted to wear, how much would cost and style matter to you? Explain your answer.

3. What kind of smart clothing would you like to see developed in the future? Why?

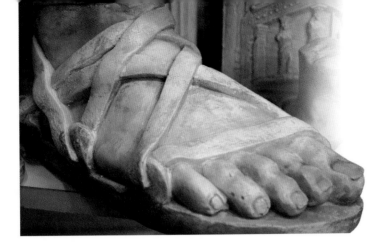

Shoes

Thinking About What You Know

Mark each statement *T* (true) or *F* (false). Discuss your answers with a partner.

_____ 1. The only function of the earliest footwear was to protect people's feet.

_____ 2. In ancient times, shoes often showed an individual's status in society.

_____ 3. People used to wear the same-shaped shoes on their left and right foot.

_____ 4. People wore athletic shoes in the Middle Ages.

_____ 5. Until the nineteenth century, shoes were made by hand.

_____ 6. Shoes with heels did not appear until the twentieth century.

Skimming

Skim the reading to check your answers. Then read the whole text.

1   Most of us have several pairs of shoes – but have you ever wondered where shoes came from? When did people first start wearing them? And how did they evolve from something to protect our feet to fashion statement?

2   History tells us that footwear was one of the first things primitive people learned to make. Footwear helped ancient peoples cross rocky terrain or hot sands without injuring themselves. The earliest footwear we know of was simply a piece of plaited grass or leather tied to the feet.

3   The ancient Egyptians seem to have invented the first footwear with a firm sole – sandals. In those days, footwear, or lack of it, also showed a person's status. Egyptian royalty, for example, wore sandals that had a different style from those with lesser status. And slaves were not allowed to wear anything on their feet. The sandal is still the basic form of footwear in many countries, particularly those with a hot climate; whereas in cold climates, an entirely different type of shoe evolved – the moccasin – a slipper-shaped shoe made of soft but sturdy leather.

4   The Greeks were the first to develop shoes with heels. Then, in the Middle Ages, shoes with long points at the toe became very chic for

the nobility. These shoes were often very difficult to wear. Other trends followed, with square-toed shoes, wide shoes, and even shoes that could make a woman stand two feet taller. Not surprisingly, these sometimes led to accidents. Even today, fashion rather than comfort often dictates the kind of shoes women wear.

5   Mechanical shoemaking appeared in the 1800s in North America. Until then, shoes had been made with the same kinds of hand tools used by the ancient Egyptians. Now it was possible to make shoes that were shaped to fit either the left or right foot. And in 1858, a machine was invented that could stitch the sole of a shoe to the upper part. Toward the end of the 1800s came a new type of shoe that was specifically designed for sports – the sneaker – and it soon become an all-time favorite.

6   The father of the modern athletic shoe was Adolf Dassler, who began making shoes in 1920. In 1948, he founded the Adidas company, one of the best-known makers of contemporary athletic shoes. Nike, Puma, New Balance, and Reebok are other examples of companies that compete for prominence in the huge market for athletic shoes today.

7   In today's competitive marketplace, every shoe company wants its styles to be unique and fashionable. Each new season, people visit stores and Web sites to see displays of the latest styles for all types of shoes: slippers, sandals, dress shoes, casual shoes, boots, as well as athletic shoes. Among the many choices are also shoes designed by internationally famous designers, such as Manolo Blahnik and Jimmy Choo. These two highly successful shoe designers have become celebrities in the world of fashion.

8   Clearly, shoes are no longer just foot protection. From decorative shoes that denoted nobility to the enormous popularity of celebrity shoe designers today, shoes are now more than ever an integral part of our ability to express our fashion sense and individuality.

A Comprehension Check

Put the events in the correct order from _1_ (the earliest) to _8_ (the most recent).

_____ a. People wore sandals for the first time.

_____ b. People wore square-toed shoes.

_____ c. Shoes were made to fit the shape of the left foot and the right foot.

_____ d. Shoes with long points at the toe became popular.

_____ e. Shoe designers became celebrities.

_____ f. Shoes with heels were introduced.

_____ g. People wore a piece of plaited grass or leather tied to their feet.

_____ h. The sports shoe became an all-time favorite.

B Vocabulary Study

Match the words from the reading that are similar in meaning.

_____ 1. *evolve* (pars. 1 & 3)   a. *simply* (par. 2)

_____ 2. *firm* (par. 3)   b. *sturdy* (par. 3)

_____ 3. *showed* (par. 3)   c. *nobility* (par. 4)

_____ 4. *royalty* (par. 3)   d. *develop* (par. 4)

_____ 5. *chic* (par. 4)   e. *fashionable* (par. 7)

_____ 6. *just* (par. 8)   f. *denoted* (par. 8)

C Understanding Text Organization

> In a well-organized text, related topics are grouped together and presented in a logical sequence. If you understand how a text is organized, it will be easier to understand the ideas.

Write the correct paragraph number or numbers next to each topic from the reading. (Note: You will use each paragraph number once.)

_5_ a. describes an advance in the way shoes are made

_____ b. discusses the current state of the market for shoes

_____ c. restates and expands on the main idea

_____ d. describes the first forms of footwear

_____ e. presents the main idea of the reading

_____ f. discusses a modern type of shoe that has become extremely popular

_____ g. describes the first shoes that people wore to be fashionable

Now complete the diagram with the correct letters to see the logical sequence of ideas.

☐ → ☐ → ☐ → *a* → ☐ → ☐ → ☐

D Relating Reading to Personal Experience

Discuss these questions with your classmates.

1. Can people's shoes tell you something about them? Explain your answer.

2. What customs associated with shoes are there in different parts of the world?

3. What technological developments would you like to see in shoes of the future? For example, would you like shoes that never wear out?

Style, Not Fashion

Thinking About the Topic

Check (✓) the statements you agree with. Discuss your answers with a partner.

_____ 1. Unlike fashion, a sense of style comes from within you.

_____ 2. Fashion and style are the same thing.

_____ 3. You can't have style without being fashionable.

_____ 4. In order to have style, you need to have money.

_____ 5. If you have a large wardrobe, you have style.

_____ 6. Status symbols are an important part of having style.

Skimming

Skim the reading to check which statements the writer agrees with. Then read the whole text.

1   Style goes way beyond fashion; it is the distinctive way we put ourselves together. It is a unique blend of spirit and substance – personal identity imposed on, and created through, the world of things. It is a way of capturing something vibrant, making a statement about ourselves in clothes. It is what people really want when they aspire to be fashionable (if they aren't just adorning themselves in status symbols).

2   Through clothes, we reinvent ourselves every time we get dressed. Our wardrobe is our visual vocabulary. Style is our distinctive pattern of speech, our individual poetry.

3   Fashion is the least of it. Style is, for starters, one part identity: self-awareness and self-knowledge. You can't have style until you have a sense of who you are. And style

requires security – feeling at home in your body, physically and mentally. Of course, like all knowledge, self-knowledge must be updated as you grow and evolve; style takes ongoing self-assessment.

Style is also one part personality: spirit, verve, attitude, wit, inventiveness. It demands the desire and confidence to express whatever mood one wishes. Such variability is not only necessary but a reflection of a person's unique complexity as a human being. People want to be themselves and to be seen as themselves. In order to work, style must reflect the *real* self, the character and personality of the individual; anything less appears to be a costume. 4

Lastly, style is one part fashion. It's possible to have lots of clothes and not an ounce of style. But it's also possible to have very few clothes and lots of style. Yes, fashion is the means through which we express style, but it takes fewer clothes to be stylish than you might imagine. 5

Whatever else it is, style is optimism made visible. Style presumes that you are a person of interest, that the world is a place of interest, that life is worth making the effort for. It also shows that you are morally responsible. It shows that you don't buy things at the whim of the marketplace or the urging of marketers. Rather, you focus on what is personally suitable and expressive. 6

Style exposes people's ambivalence[1] over good looks. It always demonstrates that appearances do count. Deep down we suspect this, since we ourselves make judgments about others from how they look. 7

No one should be penalized for not having style, of course, but those who have it are distinctive and thus more memorable. They create a unique identity for themselves and express it through grooming and a few well-chosen clothes. They announce to the world that they are in command of themselves. 8

_____

[1] *ambivalence:* having two opposing feelings at the same time

Adapted from *Psychology Today*

A Comprehension Check

Every paragraph in the reading has one main idea. Write the correct paragraph number for each main idea.

_____ a. Fashion is part of style.

_____ b. In order to have style, you have to know who you are.

_____ c. Style indicates that people pay attention to appearances.

_____ d. You notice people with style more than people without style.

_____ e. Your style shows your personality.

_____ f. Style is a mix of our inner world and the world outside ourselves.

_____ g. Through style, we can continuously change who we are.

_____ h. Style has a positive effect on individuals and society.

B Vocabulary Study

Find the words or phrases in the reading that match these definitions. The number of blanks represents the number of words in the answer.

1. forced _____ (par. 1)

2. full of life _____ (par. 1)

3. being comfortable _____ _____ _____ (par. 3)

4. made more modern or appropriate _____ (par. 3)

5. continuous _____ (par. 3)

6. way _____ (par. 5)

7. are important _____ (par. 7)

8. making your appearance clean and neat _____ (par. 8)

C Interpreting Metaphorical Language

> A metaphor is an expression that describes one thing by referring to something else with the same characteristics. If we say someone has a "heart of stone," for example, we mean the person is not emotional, kind, or compassionate. Writers sometimes use metaphorical language to intensify their meaning and encourage readers to take a fresh look at the person, object, or topic being discussed.

Work with a partner and discuss what the writer means by the following examples of metaphorical language.

1. Our wardrobe is our visual vocabulary. (par. 2)

2. Style is our individual poetry. (par. 2)

3. Style is optimism made visible. (par. 6)

D Relating Reading to Personal Experience

Discuss these questions with your classmates.

1. Do you think it is true, as the article states, that we "make judgments about others from how they look"? Give examples.

2. What does your style of dress say about your personality?

3. Do you think style is, or should be, equally important for males and females? Why or why not?

> Reread one of the unit readings and time yourself. Note your reading speed in the chart on page 124.

UNIT 10 The Media

Look at the titles of the readings and their brief descriptions to preview this unit's content. Before you begin each reading, answer the questions about it.

Reading 1 ▶ ## Youth and the News Media

Today people have a lot of choice in how they get the news. In this article, you will learn the results of a survey that examines how young people choose to get their news.

1. Do you think it's important to stay up-to-date with the news? Why or why not? Do you consider yourself well informed about current events?

2. How often do you read a newspaper or news magazine?

3. Which type of news are you most interested in – local, regional, national, or international? Are you more interested in entertainment news or sports news?

Reading 2 ▶ ## When Our Worlds Collide

What are the ethical issues that photographers and photo editors face in mainstream journalism? This magazine article looks at some of the issues.

1. When you flip through a newspaper or a magazine, what do you usually notice first?

2. What are the most popular subjects of newspaper and magazine photos?

3. How are the pictures in newspapers different from those in celebrity magazines?

Reading 3 ▶ ## Media Violence

This excerpt from a book presents opposing views on media violence.

1. Where do you most often see violence in the media: on the Internet, in video games, on TV, or in the movies?

2. Do violent movies and TV shows bother you? Why or why not?

3. Have you seen a violent movie or TV program recently? If so, did it have any effect on your mood or behavior?

Youth and the News Media

Predicting

Work with a partner. Look at the title and the opening sentence of each paragraph. Then predict how these three questions will be answered.

1. Do people in their teens and twenties often read newspapers?

2. What kinds of media are people in their teens and twenties most interested in?

3. What kinds of news are men interested in? What kinds of news interest women?

Skimming

Skim the reading to check your predictions. Then read the whole text.

1   Publishers are increasingly concerned about declining rates of newspaper readership among young people. A recent study looked at youth and the news media in 10 countries (the United States, the United Kingdom, Serbia, Sweden, Spain, Lebanon, South Africa, Colombia, the Philippines, and Japan). Researchers asked 10 young people in each country to document their media habits and attitudes. Here are some patterns that the researchers found.

2 **Young people get news from many media sources.** Many survey participants said that having detailed knowledge about the news is important. They believe that being well informed requires seeking out multiple news sources, and they feel uncomfortable trusting a single source. Other participants said the use of multiple sources and formats is a matter of convenience. Online sources, for example, are more easily accessible during the day, whereas newspapers are usually found in the morning, and TV is more accessible at night.

3 **Young people want to interact with the news media.** Almost all participants said they want an interactive experience with the media they consume. Control over the information they receive and its format is becoming more desirable, even in countries with lower Internet usage rates. As one participant said, ". . .with the Internet, you can pick whatever you want and find information that you're interested in instead of having the news dictate what's important for you."

Young people spend more time with new media than with traditional media. 4
Usage of new media where available (computers, cell phones, the Internet, and MP3 players) is increasingly taking up young people's media time. Despite this, many participants said that if they had more time, they would like to read newspapers. Traditional sources of information, such as newspapers and television, are still perceived by many participants to be more accurate, reliable, and trustworthy. Few dismiss them as obsolete.

Being well informed is a desirable quality for youth. Many participants say they 5
see a link between keeping up-to-date with current events and being able to participate in conversations with their peers and family. In addition, many participants noted that "being well informed" was beneficial at school and work, allowing them to participate in discussions and showcase their knowledge.

Youth are not only interested in local news and content that is relevant to 6
their lives. Participants said they were also curious about local, regional, national, and international news. One participant put it this way: "Nowadays a lot of people know a lot of things, so to be competitive, you also have to know a lot of things." There was also a sense among participants that local and international issues are increasingly linked, especially in relation to environmental and global issues.

Age and gender impact the news interests of young people. Younger participants 7
were more interested in "the big headlines," while older participants had more appetite for details and debate. While most participants said they usually read "the front page" of the newspaper, almost everyone said they usually ignore the business section because "it's not really eye-catching or thrilling reading." Females were more likely to read the entertainment sections of newspapers and ignore the sports sections; the reverse was true for males.

The biggest competition for news and information in the future are young people 8
themselves and their social networks. The importance of the social network as a disseminator of news and information is on the rise. Many participants listed "discussion with friends" as a top source for news and information, sometimes ranking higher than TV or newspapers. In particular, social networks appear to be key in spreading entertainment news for most young people.

Adapted from http://www.wan-press.org/IMG/pdf/Youth_Media_DNA.pdf

A Comprehension Check

Look at the example. Then find and correct six more mistakes in this paragraph.

A survey of ~~ten~~ young people showed that youth get their news from a variety of
100
sources. Very few young people want to interact with the news media, so they mostly
use cell phones and newspapers. Most of them think traditional news sources are
less accurate than new media sources. Researchers also found that young people are
interested in local news but not global news. Age and gender seem to have a small
effect on their specific interests. Finally, the survey showed that social networks are
not an important source of news for young people.

B Vocabulary Study

Find the words in the box in the reading. Then complete the sentences.

declining (par. 1)	taking up (par. 4)	perceived (par. 4)
peers (par. 5)	ignore (par. 7)	disseminator (par. 8)

1. Which activity is _____ more of your time these days: reading books or surfing the Internet?

2. Do your parents' _____ read the newspaper every day, or do people their age use the Internet instead?

3. Do you pay attention to details in the news, or do you _____ them?

4. Is the number of sports articles in the news _____ or going up?

5. Do you think TV is the most popular _____ of information?

6. Are Internet news articles _____ by your friends to be accurate?

C Thinking Beyond the Text

> Good readers are able to go beyond the words that a writer actually uses and understand ideas that are never directly expressed. One way to practice this strategy is to imagine other information that the writer could have added about the topic.

Read the following quotes. If these quotes had been included in the reading, in which paragraph would you expect to find each one?

_____ a. "Economic problems in another country may affect my ability to find a job."

_____ b. "My dad reads every section of the paper. I only read the front page."

_____ c. "I like using the Net because I can read people's comments and post my own. You can't do that with a newspaper."

_____ d. "Most of the time, I hear the latest news from my friends."

_____ e. "I don't want to be influenced by the ideas in just one source of news."

_____ f. "I don't have time to read a newspaper from cover to cover, but I'd like to."

D Relating Reading to Personal Experience

Discuss these questions with your classmates.

1. Which parts of the reading are true for you regarding how you get the news?

2. Are your news interests similar to or different from the interests of other members of your family? Do you get the news in similar or different ways? Explain.

3. Do you think newspapers will die out in the future? Why or why not?

When Our Worlds Collide

Predicting

Work with a partner. Look at the title and the pictures. Who are the people? What are they doing? Write a caption for each picture.

Picture 1: _____

Picture 2: _____

Skimming

Skim the first paragraph and the last paragraph. Check to see if your captions are appropriate. Then read the whole text.

"Wanna buy a body?" That was the opening line of more than a few phone calls I got   1
from freelance photographers when I was a photo editor at *U.S. News*. Like many in the
mainstream press, I wanted to separate the world of photographers into "them," who trade
in pictures of bodies or chase celebrities, and "us," the serious news people. But after 16
years in that role, I came to wonder whether the two worlds were easily distinguishable.

Working in the reputable world of journalism, I assigned photographers to cover other   2
people's nightmares. I justified invading moments of grief, under the guise of the reader's
right to know. I didn't ask photographers to trespass or to stalk, but I didn't have to: I
worked with pros who did what others did: talking their way into situations or shooting
from behind police lines to get pictures I was after. And I wasn't alone.

In the aftermath of a car crash or some other hideous incident when ordinary people   3
are hurt or killed, you rarely see photographers pushing, paparazzi-like, past rescue
workers to capture the blood and gore. But you are likely to see local newspaper and
television photographers on the scene – and fast. Photographs of the latest emergencies
are an important part of news coverage.

4   How can we justify our behavior? Journalists are taught to separate doing the job from worrying about the consequences of publishing what they record. Repeatedly, they are reminded of a news-business dictum: Leave your conscience in the office. You get the picture or the footage; the decision whether to print or air it comes later. A victim may lie bleeding, unconscious, or dead: Your job is to record the image. You're a photographer, not a paramedic. You put away your emotions and document the scene.

5   We act this way partly because we know that the pictures can have important meaning. Photographs can change deplorable situations by mobilizing public outrage or increasing public understanding.

6   However, catastrophic events often bring out the worst in photographers and photo editors. In the first minutes and hours after a disaster occurs, photo agencies buy pictures. They rush to obtain exclusive rights to dramatic images, and death is usually the subject. Often an agency buys a picture from a local newspaper or an amateur photographer and puts it up for bid by major magazines. The most keenly sought "exclusives" command tens of thousands of dollars through bidding contests.

7   I worked on many stories of disastrous events. When they happen, you move quickly: buying, dealing, assigning, trying to beat the agencies to the pictures. I rarely felt the impact of the story, at least until the coverage was over.

8   Many people believe that journalists need to change the way they do things, and it's our pictures that annoy people the most. Readers may not believe, as we do, that there is a distinction between sober-minded "us" and sleazy "them." In too many cases, by our choices of images as well as how we get them, we prove our readers right.

Adapted from *U.S. News & World Report*

A Comprehension Check

Mark each statement *T* (true) or *F* (false). Then correct the false statements.

_____ 1. The writer never got an offer for a photograph of a dead person.

_____ 2. The writer told himself that taking pictures of people's suffering was his way of informing the public.

_____ 3. Journalists covering a news story aren't supposed to think about whether they are doing the right thing.

_____ 4. News photographers are usually a problem for rescue workers at an accident.

_____ 5. Sometimes journalists can help people by showing certain photographs.

_____ 6. Editors pay a lot of money for pictures that their competitors want.

_____ 7. The writer was strongly affected by the news story while he was working on the pictures for it.

_____ 8. Much of the public does not think people in the news business do the right thing.

B Vocabulary Study

Find the words in the reading that match these definitions.

1. recognized as different _____ (par. 1)

2. to illegally follow and watch someone _____ (par. 2)

3. terrible _____ (par. 3)

4. photographers who chase celebrities _____ (par. 3)

5. show that something is reasonable or right _____ (par. 4)

6. a person who gives emergency medical help _____ (par. 4)

7. extreme anger _____ (par. 5)

8. not morally acceptable _____ (par. 8)

C Recognizing Point of View

> Sometimes a writer expresses a point of view, or an opinion. An important part of reading critically is being able to recognize the presence of a point of view and determining what that point of view is.

Check (✓) the statement that best expresses the writer's point of view about photographers in the news business. Compare your answer with a partner. Identify the parts of the reading that support your choice.

_____ 1. The writer believes that photographers in the news business are more ethical than photographers who chase celebrities.

_____ 2. The writer believes that photographers in the news business should leave their consciences at the office.

_____ 3. The writer believes that photographers in the news business should change the way they do their job.

D Relating Reading to Personal Experience

Discuss these questions with your classmates.

1. Why do you think photographs play an important role in telling a news story? Think of a picture that had a strong impact on you, and tell the class about it.

2. Do the newspapers you read print pictures of catastrophic events? Do you think they should? Why or why not?

3. Do you think journalism is a respectable profession? Why or why not?

Media Violence

Predicting

Look at the title of the reading and read these excerpts. Then, look at the two subheads. Decide which part of the reading each excerpt comes from: 1 or 2. Compare your answers with a partner.

____ 1. . . . heavy exposure to televised violence is one of the causes of aggressive behavior . . .

____ 2. Parents worried about the impact culture has on their kids should ignore the headlines . . .

____ 3. . . . sometimes these [violent] images help the child to sort matters out . . .

____ 4. Parents are confronting the fact that the real story about media violence . . . has been withheld.

Skimming

Skim the reading to check your predictions. Then read the whole text.

Media violence harms children

1   The debate is over. Violence on television and in the movies is damaging to children. Forty years of research concludes that repeated exposure to high levels of media violence teaches some children and adolescents to settle interpersonal differences with violence while teaching many more to be indifferent to this solution. Under the media's influence, children at younger and younger ages are using violence as a first, not a last, resort to conflict.

2   Locked away in professional journals are thousands of articles documenting the negative effects of media, particularly media violence, on our nation's youth. Children who are heavy viewers of television are more aggressive, more pessimistic, weigh more, are less imaginative, and less capable students than their lighter-viewing counterparts. With an increasing sense of urgency, parents are confronting the fact that the "real story" about media violence and its effects on children has been withheld.

3   Leonard Eron, one of the most important experts on media and children in the United States, has said that:

> There can no longer be any doubt that heavy exposure to televised violence is one of the causes of aggressive behavior, crime, and violence in society. The

evidence comes from both the laboratory and real-life studies. Television   4
violence affects youngsters of all ages, of both genders, at all socioeconomic
levels, and all levels of intelligence. The effect is not limited to children who
are already disposed to being aggressive and is not restricted to this country.

Every major group concerned with children has studied and issued reports on the   4
effects of media violence on children. Many have called for curbing television and movie
violence. Doctors, therapists, teachers, and youth workers all find themselves struggling
to help youngsters who, influenced by repeated images of violence, find it increasingly
difficult to deal with the inevitable frustrations of daily life.

Media violence does not harm children

We often have trouble understanding the complicated connections between culture   5
and violence. One of the reasons is that so many "experts" are thrown at us, often offering
contradictory conclusions.

Some experts, however, have better credentials than others. Harvard psychiatrist   6
Robert Coles, no fan of TV violence, has been studying and writing about the moral,
spiritual, and developmental lives of children for much of his life. His works have been
widely praised and circulated as new, insightful looks at kids' complex inner lives. Parents
worried about the impact culture has on their kids should ignore the headlines and read
Coles's book, *The Moral Life of Children*. They would know more and feel better.

A young moviegoer, Coles writes, can repeatedly be exposed to the "excesses of a   7
Hollywood genre" – sentimentality, violence, the misrepresentation of history, racial
stereotypes, pure simplemindedness – and emerge unharmed intellectually as well as
morally. In fact, sometimes these images help the child to "sort matters out, stop and
think about what is true and what is not by any means true." The child, says Coles,
"doesn't forget what he's learned in school, learned at home, from hearing people talk in
his family and his neighborhood."

Culture offers important moments for moral reflection, and it ought not to be used   8
as an occasion for "overwrought psychiatric comment," Coles warns, or for making
simpleminded connections between films and "the collective American conscience."

Adapted from *Media Violence: Opposing Viewpoints*

A Comprehension Check

**Write one check (✓) next to the statement that best expresses the main idea of the
first part of the reading. Write two checks (✓✓) next to the statement that best
expresses the main idea of the second part.**

_____ 1. A lot more research on the subject of media violence is still needed.

_____ 2. An expert's studies have led some people to worry less about media violence.

_____ 3. Experts overwhelmingly agree that media violence has harmful effects.

_____ 4. Parents want to know about the effects media violence has on their children.

_____ 5. The media influences children more than their parents or teachers do.

B Vocabulary Study

Find the words in *italics* in the reading. Then match the words with their meanings.

_____ 1. *settle differences* (par. 1)   a. showing clear understanding

_____ 2. *indifferent to* (par. 1)   b. likely to

_____ 3. *last resort* (par. 1)   c. end arguments

_____ 4. *disposed to* (par. 3)   d. only remaining choice

_____ 5. *curbing* (par. 4)   e. unconcerned about

_____ 6. *credentials* (par. 6)   f. ability and experience

_____ 7. *insightful* (par. 6)   g. reducing

C Making Inferences

> Sometimes the reader must infer, or figure out, what the writer did not explain or state directly in the text.

Who would have said each of the following statements? Write *LE* (Leonard Eron) or *RC* (Robert Coles). Compare your answers with a partner.

_____ 1. Movies influence children less than their families and friends do.

_____ 2. Psychiatrists are overreacting to violence in the media.

_____ 3. Seeing violence on TV definitely makes kids more aggressive.

_____ 4. Watching violent scenes can help children distinguish fantasy from reality.

_____ 5. Children from different backgrounds are all harmed by violence on TV.

_____ 6. Media violence affects both boys and girls.

D Relating Reading to Personal Experience

Discuss these questions with your classmates.

1. Do you think media violence is harmful to children and adolescents? Why or why not?

2. At what age would you allow children to watch violent TV programs and movies? Explain your answer.

3. Do you think video games have a positive or negative effect on children? Why?

> **Reread one of the unit readings and time yourself. Note your reading speed in the chart on page 124.**

UNIT 11 Art

Look at the titles of the readings and their brief descriptions to preview this unit's content. Before you begin each reading, answer the questions about it.

Reading 1

Girl with a Pitcher

This excerpt from a novel reveals how one artist sees and describes the colors he uses to paint.

1. Name a famous painting that you know and then try to visualize it. What colors do you see?

2. Look out the window. What colors do you see?

3. Imagine that you are an artist's helper. What tasks do you think the artist would have you do?

Reading 2

Organic Architecture

In this newspaper article, learn about an architectural movement that draws inspiration from the beauty and harmony of nature.

1. Describe the shapes of the buildings in a place where you live or have lived in the past. Are the structures mostly made up of straight lines, or do many of them have curves?

2. Where do you think an architect could find inspiration for new designs?

3. What features do you think characterize "good architecture"?

Reading 3

Could You Be a Trash Artist?

Can you imagine turning something that you would normally discard into a useful or beautiful item? This article discusses that idea.

1. When you think of the word *art*, what comes to mind?

2. What do you think is the meaning of the expression: "Beauty is in the eye of the beholder"? Look around you and find something that you think is beautiful. Ask your classmates if they agree with you.

3. What household items, other than food, do you normally throw away? How could you reuse them?

Girl with a Pitcher

Predicting

Look carefully at the picture. What colors did the artist use to paint the different parts of the picture listed below? Choose from the list in the box. Compare your answers with a partner.

a. black	e. gray	i. white
b. blue	f. yellow	j. yellow ocher[1]
c. brown	g. red	
d. green	h. silver	

1. the girl's skirt: _____

2. the wall behind the girl: _____

3. the pitcher and basin: _____

[1] *yellow ocher:* yellow orange

Johannes Vermeer (Dutch, 1632–1675),
Young Woman with a Pitcher, 1664–1665

Scanning

Scan the reading to find the colors the artist used to paint the items above.

1   He began the painting of the baker's daughter with a layer of pale gray on the white canvas. After that I thought he would begin to paint what he saw. Instead he painted patches of color. They were the wrong colors – none was the color of the thing itself. He spent a long time on these false colors, as I call them.

2   I reluctantly set out the colors he asked for each morning. One day I put out a blue as well. The second time I laid it out he said to me, "No ultramarine, Griet. Only the colors I asked for. Why did you set it out when I did not ask for it?" He was annoyed.

3   "I'm sorry, sir. It's just –" I took a deep breath – "she is wearing a blue skirt. I thought you would want it, rather than leaving it black."

4   "When I am ready, I will ask."

5   I nodded and turned back to polishing the lion-head chair. My chest hurt. I did not want him to be angry at me.

6   He opened the middle window, filling the room with cold air.

7   "Come here, Griet."

8   I set my rag on the sill and went to him.

"Look out the window." 9

I looked out. It was a breezy day, with clouds disappearing behind the New 10
Church tower.

"What color are those clouds?" 11

"Why, white, sir." 12

He raised his eyebrows slightly. "Are they?" 13

I glanced at them. "And gray. Perhaps it will snow." 14

"Come, Griet, you can do better than that. Think of your vegetables." 15

"My vegetables, sir?" 16

He moved his head slightly. I was annoying him again. My jaw tightened. 17

"Think of how you separated the whites. Your turnips and your onions – are they the 18
same white?"

Suddenly I understood. "No. The turnip has green in it, the onion yellow." 19

"Exactly. Now, what colors do you see in the clouds?" 20

"There is some blue in them," I said after studying them for a few minutes. "And – 21
yellow as well. And there is some green!" I became so excited I actually pointed. I
had been looking at clouds all my life, but I felt as if I saw them for the first time at
that moment.

He smiled. "You will find there is little pure white in clouds, yet people say they are 22
white. Now do you understand why I do not need the blue yet?"

"Yes, sir." I did not really understand, but did not want to admit it. I felt I almost knew. 23

When at last he began to add colors on top of the false colors, I saw what he meant. 24
He painted a light blue over the girl's skirt, and it became a blue through which bits of
black could be seen, darker in the shadow of the table, lighter closer to the window. To
the wall areas he added yellow ocher, through which some of the gray showed. It became
a bright but not a white wall. When the light shone on the wall, I discovered, it was not
white, but many colors.

The pitcher and basin were the most complicated – they became yellow, and brown, 25
and green, and blue. They reflected the pattern of the rug, the girl's bodice, the blue cloth
draped over the chair – everything but their true silver color. And yet they looked as they
should, like a pitcher and a basin.

After that I could not stop looking at things. 26

From *Girl with a Pearl Earring*

A Comprehension Check

Mark each statement *T* (true) or *F* (false). Then correct the false statements.

_____ 1. Griet was happy to lay out the painter's colors every morning.

_____ 2. At first, the painter did not want blue paint for the blue skirt.

_____ 3. Griet apologized for putting out blue paint.

_____ 4. When Griet first looked at the clouds, she said they were gray.

_____ 5. Griet had always paid attention to the way things looked.

_____ 6. By adding different colors to an object, the painter made it look more real.

B Vocabulary Study

Find the words in the box in the reading. Then complete the sentences.

layer (par. 1)	pale (par. 1)	patches (par. 1)
rag (par. 8)	shadow (par. 24)	draped (par. 25)

1. On a sunny day, you can see your _____ on the sidewalk.

2. The painting was mostly black and gray, but there were a few _____ of red.

3. She wore her bright yellow dress, not the _____ yellow one.

4. He waited until the first _____ of paint dried before applying the second one.

5. He used a _____ to wipe the paint off his hands.

6. She had a blanket _____ over her knees because she was cold.

C Making Inferences

> Sometimes the reader must infer, or figure out, what the writer does not explain or state directly in the text.

Answer the questions with a partner. Explain the reasons for your answers.

1. Who is Griet?

2. What kind of person is Griet?

3. What kind of person is the artist?

4. Why did the artist tell Griet she could "do better than that"? (par. 15)

5. Why does Griet say she "could not stop looking at things" after that? (par. 26)

D Relating Reading to Personal Experience

Discuss these questions with your classmates.

1. Who is your favorite artist? What do you like about the artist's work?

2. What colors would you use to paint a picture of the place where you are now?

3. Has anyone ever changed the way you look at art or nature? If so, how did it happen and how did your perception change?

Organic Architecture

1

Previewing Vocabulary

According to the reading, architects can be inspired by the following:

driftwood	the swirls of a mollusk	a prehistoric bird
a giant fungus	the shape of a turtle	the body of a salmon

Work with a partner. Discuss the meaning of the words and look at the pictures. Then write what you think *organic architecture* means.

Skimming

Skim the reading to check your answer. Then read the whole text.

When architect Douglas Cardinal was studying at the University of Texas many years ago, he used to drive to the college through the Rocky Mountains from his home in Alberta, Canada. "I took a new route every time and was inspired by those forms," Cardinal told an American journalist. "They helped me realize architecture should stem from the natural environment of a place." 1

While Canadians are familiar with Cardinal's highly original work, he is not alone in taking inspiration from nature and preferring curves to straight lines. As a key contributor to an international movement known as organic architecture, Cardinal has had his work and views prominently featured in *The New Organic Architecture: The Breaking Wave* by British architect David Pearson. There is no simple definition of *organic architecture*. But in his book, Pearson attempts to convey the meaning of the term with examples of fascinating buildings by 30 contemporary architects from 15 countries. 2

3   These imaginative structures share common characteristics: They draw inspiration from natural forms and strive to apply ecological science to how the buildings are lit, heated, and cooled. They harmonize with the landscape and express the human spirit.

4   For example, on the South Pacific island of New Caledonia, Italian architect Renzo Piano has designed a stunning jungle village inspired by native huts and their relationship to nature. These mysterious, soaring wood structures resemble wicker baskets or giant curved barrels, and are designed for natural ventilation.

5   In Palm Springs, California, American architect Kendrick Bangs Kellogg has created a desert house whose roof canopies resemble a giant fungus. From another angle, its curved concrete wings make the house look like a prehistoric bird rising from the landscape. The house is earthquake-proof and captures and stores the sun's heat, releasing it at night.

6   "There's a growing awareness of the need for all architects to impact as little as possible on the environment," Pearson said in an interview from his London office. "What is new is to link the newer environmental awareness to the passionate design that can come out of looking at nature and its forms."

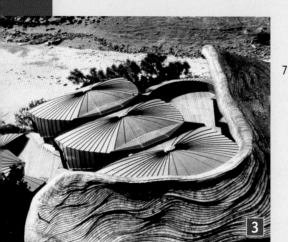

7   Pearson is reminded of the natural world in a wide range of remarkable buildings that demonstrate the diversity of the organic approach; he sees it in the winglike detail of the spire of a Roman Catholic church in Hungary by Imre Makovecz; the extraordinary bubble-shaped domes of the new Eden Project botanical center in Cornwall, England, by Nicholas Grimshaw; and, again, in an ocean-view California house by Bart Prince that sprawls like an exquisite piece of driftwood.

8   "Organic architecture is rooted in a passion for life, nature, and natural forms," Pearson writes. "Emphasizing beauty and harmony, its free-flowing curves and expressive forms are sympathetic to the human body, mind, and spirit. In a well-designed 'organic' building, we feel better and freer."

9   Cardinal has won an award for a turtle-shaped civic center, and he has also designed an interpretive center[1] for the site of a 9,000-year-old village in British Columbia. The shape of the interpretive center suggests the curving body of a salmon, the swirls of a mollusk, and wavy patterns of sand created by tides.

10   "There's an infinite variety of forms in nature, and I am continually inspired by observing all these forms," says Cardinal.

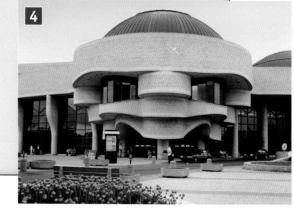

---

[1] *interpretive center:* a kind of museum that informs visitors about a place through a variety of media such as video and interactive exhibits

Adapted from *The Ottawa Citizen*

A Comprehension Check

Complete the paragraph about organic architecture with words from the box.

ecology	natural forms	turtle-shaped	sun	wings	ventilation

Organic architecture draws inspiration from _____. Two good examples are
1

Cardinal's _____ civic center and Kellogg's Palm Springs house with curved
2

concrete _____. Another key feature of organic architecture is that it applies
3

_____ to the heating, cooling, and lighting of buildings. For example, Piano's
4

wooden houses in New Caledonia are designed for natural _____, and
5

Kellogg's house saves energy by storing the heat of the _____.
6

B Vocabulary Study

Cross out the word in each row that doesn't belong to the category in bold. If necessary, look back at the reading to see how the words are used.

1. **architecture words**   canopy   dome   spire   landscape
2. **geography words**   desert   jungle   village   mountains
3. **words about origin**   stem from   rooted in   come out of   harmonize with
4. **environment words**   nature   expressive   organic   botanical
5. **building words**   hut   structure   church   tides

C Organizing Information into a Chart

> Organizing information into a chart can help you deepen your understanding of a reading and see how different parts of the reading relate to each other.

Complete the chart with information about each structure.

	Picture 1	Picture 2	Picture 3	Picture 4
a. Architect	Renzo Piano			
b. Location				
c. Resembles				

D Relating Reading to Personal Experience

Discuss these questions with your classmates.

1. Which of the structures in the pictures do you like best? Why?

2. Are there any examples of organic architecture in your country? If so, where? If not, which of the buildings described in the reading would best fit in where you live?

3. What instructions would you give an architect to design your ideal home?

Could You Be a Trash Artist?

Thinking About the Topic

Read the list of objects below. The words are all from the reading. Discuss the meanings with a partner. Then decide which objects could be created out of (1) empty metal cans, (2) old boxes, or (3) old clothing. Write *1*, *2*, or *3* on the lines.

_____ bird feeders   _____ metal cases

_____ hanging organizers   _____ rag rugs

_____ hats   _____ storage containers

_____ forts for kids to play in   _____ vests

Skimming

Skim the reading to find the writer's suggestions for reusing cans, boxes, and clothing instead of discarding them. Then read the whole text.

1   Where some people see trash, others see art. And, in some art, some people will only see a pile of meaningless trash. So, what's the difference? Maybe it's just in the eye of the beholder or artist. Maybe it's simply a matter of opening our minds to new and unique ways of doing and seeing things. If we just looked at the world around us, we could see the potential in many of the items we carelessly discard each and every day.

2   German artist HA Schult is an example of a contemporary artist who makes use of trash on a grand scale. "We are living in the time of garbage," says Schult. "I created a

thousand sculptures of garbage. They are a mirror of ourselves." Here, Schult is referring to his 1,000 trash people, humanoids he has created from trash. He first exhibited them in 1996 in the western German state of North Rhine-Westphalia. The figures triggered such an overwhelmingly positive response that he decided to take them on tour. "It is a social sculpture," he explains. "It is not only a sculpture for the eyes. It's a sculpture to spread the idea that we live in a time of garbage." So far, Schult's social sculpture has been displayed in Paris, in Moscow's Red Square, on the Great Wall of China, and in the desert next to the Giza pyramids near Cairo.

HA Schult's work is unforgettable. Somehow its impact stays engraved in your mind.   3
Yet, despite the influence his work has had on the art world, Schult remains humble about his installations:[1] "Artists have to learn every time; that is their profession. We are not important. All that is important is the time in which we are living."

Trash art has been around for years, and it seems to make a comeback from time   4
to time. But it seems that only the more eccentric or popular artists are viewed as true artists when working with items normally discarded in the trash pile. Why can't average people be considered artists when they pull the same items out and mold them into some form of personal art of their own creating? Maybe it's because we all have our own pre-set ideas of what art is and isn't, or who artists are or should be.

Take metal cans, for instance, and imagine them in any number of uses, functional or   5
purely as an art form. Can your eyes and mind see the potential metal case, bird feeder, or other object in the simple cast off items? What about boxes or clothing? What might be done with these? Boxes can usually serve as new storage containers, and almost always serve as very imaginative forts for the kids, not to mention makeshift shelters for pets. And clothing? Imagine taking old clothes and turning them into vests, hats, hanging organizers, or rag rugs. The only limit to using these items in other ways is one's individual creativity and daringness to try.

---

[1] *installation:* a work of art, usually consisting of multiple parts, that is
constructed at the site of its exhibition

Adapted from http://www.essortment.com/all/trash_rgnv.htm
and http://www.inspiredminds.de/detail.php?id=28

A Comprehension Check

Every paragraph in the reading has one main idea. Write the correct paragraph number for each main idea. Then check (✓) the statement that best expresses the main idea of the whole reading.

_____ a. If you are creative, you can find different uses for things you normally discard.

_____ b. Some people see art where others see trash.

_____ c. HA Schult is well known for the art he has created from trash.

_____ d. We should open our minds to new ideas about art and artists.

_____ e. Trash can be changed into art, and anyone can be a trash artist.

_____ f. Schult does not think his art is as important as others may say it is.

B Vocabulary Study

Find the words in *italics* in the reading. Then match the words with their meanings.

____ 1. *triggered* (par. 2)   a. shape

____ 2. *impact* (par. 3)   b. strange or unusual

____ 3. *engraved* (par. 3)   c. very difficult to forget

____ 4. *humble* (par. 3)   d. caused something to start

____ 5. *eccentric* (par. 4)   e. powerful effect

____ 6. *mold* (par. 4)   f. not proud or not believing you are important

C Paraphrasing

> **Paraphrasing means restating what you have read in your own words. By paraphrasing parts of a text, you can deepen your understanding of it.**

Write a paraphrase of each of the following sentences from the reading.

1. Where some people see trash, others see art.

   Some people look at the things we throw out and see art.

2. German artist HA Schult is an example of a contemporary artist who makes use of trash on a grand scale.

   _____

3. Trash art has been around for years, and it seems to make a comeback from time to time.

   _____

4. The only limit to using these items in other ways is one's individual creativity.

   _____

D Relating Reading to Personal Experience

Discuss these questions with your classmates.

1. Schult says that we live in a time of garbage. What does he mean? Do you agree?

2. Do you think "trash art" is really art? Why or why not?

3. Do you think anyone can be a trash artist? Why or why not?

> **Reread one of the unit readings and time yourself. Note your reading speed in the chart on page 124.**

UNIT 12 Humor

Look at the titles of the readings and their brief descriptions to preview this unit's content. Before you begin each reading, answer the questions about it.

Reading 1 ▶ ## So, Who's the Comedian?

In this newspaper article, a man writes about his attempt to be a stand-up comic.

1. Do you like stand-up comedy? Why or why not?

2. Do you like to tell jokes? What qualities make a person a good joke teller?

3. Do you think a person can learn to have good stage presence? Why or why not?

Reading 2 ▶ ## Taking Humor Seriously in the Workplace

Does humor have a role in the workplace? According to this Internet article, humor contributes a lot to a good work environment.

1. Do you think humor can improve relationships between colleagues at work? If so, how?

2. Is it important for people to laugh at work? Why or why not?

3. Why do you think people sometimes make fun of themselves?

Reading 3 ▶ ## Three Comedians

Three well-known comedians tell funny anecdotes in this article.

1. Is stand-up comedy popular in your culture?

2. Who are your favorite comedians? Why do they make you laugh?

3. What do you think is the funniest show on TV?

So, Who's the Comedian?

Thinking About the Topic

Describe the picture. What is the man doing? Where do you think he is? Do you think he's enjoying himself? Why or why not? Discuss your answers with a partner.

Skimming

Skim the reading to find out what the writer did. Then read the whole text.

1   According to a recent poll, 84 percent of men in the United States believe they are funnier than the average stand-up comic, and that if they ever got up behind a mike, they'd bring down the house.

2   I just made up that poll, but literal truth is inessential to being a stand-up comic, which I now am. I became a stand-up comic at 12:45 yesterday afternoon when I walked onto a comedy club stage and did a "bit." It was an audition in which professional and semi-pro comedians had exactly two minutes each to perform for a big-shot producer.

3   During my two minutes, I learned many things about the craft of comedy, the main ones being:

  ◆ Two minutes is a very, very, excruciatingly long time.
  ◆ You should always remember not to put beads in your mouth, because you can die.

4   But I am getting ahead of myself.

I am not a comic, have never appeared onstage, am awkward before a mike, have no   5
spontaneity, and basically no interpersonal skills. But I have written some funny things in
the newspapers, and I figured that if you can write funny, you can be funny. That was my
first mistake.

My second mistake was not staying in my seat when my name was called. Good   6
stand-up comics hone their acts over months if not years, polishing them before
bathroom mirrors or their friends. I developed the key element of mine the morning I
went on. The last thing I did before I left the house was bring a box full of plastic beads,
because I figured they could be a prop for something.

For the first few seconds of my two minutes, I was simply staring forward, mouth   7
agape, expressing the concept: "Uuungh."

Finally I said, "This is the debut of my career as a professional stand-up comic. It's a   8
kind of a special moment for me. I'd like to take this opportunity to say something to my
mother, who was an inspiration to me throughout my life. My mother passed away a few
years ago, but I feel she is still with me. All the time, wherever I go, I feel her presence.
Day in and day out. So I would like to say this to her. LEAVE ME ALONE, MA!"

Some people actually laughed.   9

Then I said, "Anyway, this really is my first time onstage, and I'm pretty insecure   10
because, y'know, I'm not all that funny and I have a really lousy stage presence . . ."

People were laughing. Yes, I realize they were mostly laughing about how bad I was.   11

"But I've been working on the problem. A long time ago a Greek guy named   12
Demosthenes had the same problem I have, and he became a great orator by sticking
pebbles in his mouth, so I thought I would (and here I began putting the beads in my
mouth) try that. See, the idea is that if you can talk through the pebbles (now I was
stuffing them in by the handful) you can learn to . . ."

More laughter.   13

". . . talk better and wfnm fmuff frmphm grphnm fprm . . ."   14

I looked at my watch, said something that might have sounded like "My time is up,"   15
and left to somewhat spirited applause. What the audience did not know was that I was
quietly choking on a slippery bead.

Adapted from *The Washington Post*

A Comprehension Check

Check (✓) the remarks that people in the audience might have made. Discuss your choices with a partner.

_____ 1. Isn't he the guy who writes a funny newspaper column?

_____ 2. We saw that guy onstage here a couple of months ago.

_____ 3. He seemed really nervous, didn't he?

_____ 4. Wasn't that a stupid song he sang?

_____ 5. He was so terrible that it was funny.

_____ 6. Why did he talk with those things in his mouth?

B Vocabulary Study

Find the words in *italics* in the reading. Then match the words with their meanings.

_____ 1. *big-shot* (par. 2)　　　　a. lively

_____ 2. *excruciatingly* (par. 3)　　b. develop and improve

_____ 3. *awkward* (par. 5)　　　　c. painfully

_____ 4. *hone* (par. 6)　　　　　　d. important

_____ 5. *agape* (par. 7)　　　　　e. uncomfortable

_____ 6. *spirited* (par. 15)　　　　f. open wide

C Making Inferences

> Sometimes the reader must infer, or figure out, what the writer did not explain or state directly in the text.

There are four places in the reading where the writer says the audience laughed or clapped. Find each one and write brief notes to explain why they did. Compare your answers with a partner.

1. Some people actually laughed. (par. 9) _____

_____

2. People were laughing. (par. 11) _____

_____

3. More laughter. (par. 13) _____

_____

4. I . . . left to somewhat spirited applause. (par. 15) _____

_____

D Relating Reading to Personal Experience

Discuss these questions with your classmates.

1. What do you think the writer could do to improve his performance?

2. Do you think men and women are equally good as comedians? Why or why not? Do they tell jokes about the same things? Give some examples to support your answer.

3. If you were going to perform stand-up comedy, what would you talk about or do?

Taking Humor Seriously in the Workplace

Thinking About the Topic

Do you agree or disagree with these statements? Mark each statement *A* (agree) or *D* (disagree). Then discuss your answers with a partner.

_____ 1. It's a bad idea for people to use humor with their co-workers.

_____ 2. People who work together feel closer if they share jokes.

_____ 3. Laughter causes physical and psychological problems.

_____ 4. Humor helps people see their problems as less important.

_____ 5. It's good to laugh at yourself.

Skimming

Skim the reading to see if the writer agrees or disagrees with the statements above. Then read the whole text.

How important is humor in the workplace? According to human relations personnel, humor plays a critical role. In fact, when asked about the qualities of an effective employee, they say a sense of humor is a great asset. Humor in a work environment helps people get along with one another. It facilitates communication, builds relationships, reduces stress, provides perspective, and promotes attention and energy. 1

Humor facilitates communication

Another advantage of humor is that it provides a nonthreatening way for an employee or employer to communicate without putting emotional strain on the relationship. 2

Consider the frazzled office assistant who posts the sign "I have only two speeds. If this one isn't fast enough, you're not going to like my other one." Or the somewhat scattered boss whose messy desk has the sign, "A Creative Mess Is Better Than Tidy Idleness." The message is clear, yet the communication is done in a light and therefore less stressful way. The assistant's sign pokes fun at the situation, and the boss's note pokes fun at himself.

Humor builds relationships

3   Humor can facilitate staff cohesion and a sense of team effort in the workplace. Bulletin boards, electronic mail, intra-office memos, and voicemail are all mediums through which we can use humor with co-workers. Office jokes that take the seriousness of work lightly give us the opportunity to become more connected with others.

Humor reduces stress

4   Work is often associated with stress, and stress is one of the main causes of illness, absenteeism, and employee burnout. Humor helps relieve stress because it makes us feel good, and we can't feel good and feel stressed simultaneously. At the moment we experience humor, feelings like depression, anger, and anxiety dissolve. When we laugh we feel physically better, and after laughter we feel happier and more relaxed.

Humor provides perspective

5   Humor also oils the wheels of the workplace by providing perspective. Artist and author Ashleigh Brilliant (known for his one-liners on postcards) says, "Distance doesn't really make you any smaller, but it does make you part of a bigger picture." Consider the cartoon created by artist Tom Wilson. A man is lying on the psychiatrist's couch and the psychiatrist is saying, "The whole world isn't against you . . . there are BILLIONS of people who don't care one way or the other."

Humor promotes attention and energy

6   Humor also wakes us up and increases our attention. An office bulletin board full of cartoons, one-liners, jokes, and funny pictures is one way to invite humor into the workplace. A few moments of humor at work can lead to increased productivity as the newly energized employee returns to his or her task.

7   So let's take humor seriously and use it to lighten our load at work.

Adapted from www.humormatters.com/articles/workplace.htm

A Comprehension Check

Check (✓) the statement that best expresses the main idea of the reading.

_____ 1. People who take humor seriously are more effective employees.

_____ 2. Humor makes work less stressful, relationships more cohesive, and workers more productive.

_____ 3. People who have a sense of humor get along better with their co-workers.

_____ 4. Humor helps people pay careful attention at work.

_____ 5. Employees prefer bosses who have a good sense of humor.

B Vocabulary Study

Match the words from the reading that are similar in meaning.

_____ 1. *personnel* (par. 1)   a. *important* (par. 1)

_____ 2. *critical* (par. 1)   b. *advantage* (par. 2)

_____ 3. *asset* (par. 1)   c. *staff* (par. 3)

_____ 4. *frazzled* (par. 2)   d. *use humor with* (par. 3)

_____ 5. *pokes fun at* (par. 2)   e. *connected* (par. 3)

_____ 6. *associated* (par. 4)   f. *stressed* (par. 4)

_____ 7. *relieve* (par. 4)   g. *reduce* (par. 4 subheading)

C Thinking Beyond the Text

> Good readers are able to go beyond the words that a writer actually uses and understand ideas that are never directly expressed. One way to practice this strategy is to imagine other information that the writer could have added about the topic.

Read the statements about humor. If these statements were in the reading, which section would each one fit into? Write the appropriate subheading.

Humor can . . .

1. help us think about an issue in a different way. _____

2. help people enjoy spending time together. _____

3. help us deal with people who are very nervous. _____

4. help us when we're feeling tired and bored. _____

5. help a person give feedback to a co-worker. _____

D Relating Reading to Personal Experience

Discuss these questions with your classmates.

1. Can you think of a time when humor helped you and your classmates or co-workers deal with a difficult situation?

2. Do you know anyone whose sense of humor has helped them succeed? If so, tell your classmates about this person.

3. How could you introduce more humor into your classroom or workplace? Make suggestions.

Three Comedians

Predicting

A *punch line* is the last part of a joke or anecdote that makes it funny. Read the following punch lines from three comedians' anecdotes. Then answer the question below. Compare your answer with a partner.

1. Just once I would like to meet a couple that goes, "You know, we're not that happy with him, frankly. I think we really made a big mistake. We should've gotten an aquarium. You want him? We've really had enough."

2. "You don't *know* if you got a haircut? Well, tell me this: Was your head with you all day?" "I don't know," says the boy.

3. Why can't I love him from afar? That's how I want to love him – through pictures and folklore.

What topic do you think all three anecdotes are about?

Skimming

Skim the reading to check your prediction. Then read the whole text.

Jerry Seinfeld

Jerry Seinfeld

1   My friends just had a baby. There is so much pressure to see this baby. Every time I talk to them, they say, "You have got to see the baby. When are you coming over to see the baby? See the baby. See the baby."

2   Nobody ever wants you to come over and see their grandfather. "You gotta see him. He's sooo cute. A hundred and sixty-eight pounds, four ounces. I love when they're this age. He's a thousand months. You know the mid-eighties is such a good time for grandpeople. You've got to see him."

3   What's tough about seeing people when they have a new baby is that you have to try and match their level of enthusiasm. They're always so excited. "What do you think of him? What do you think?"

4   Just once I would like to meet a couple that goes, "You know, we're not that happy with him, frankly. I think we really made a big mistake. We should've gotten an aquarium. You want him? We've really had enough."

Bill Cosby

1   We parents so often blow the business of raising kids, but not because we violate any philosophy of child raising. I doubt there can *be* a philosophy about something so difficult, something so downright mystical, as raising kids. A baseball manager has

learned a lot about his job from having played the game, but a parent has not learned a thing from having once been a child. What can you learn about a business in which the child's favorite response is "I don't know"?

A father enters his son's room and sees that the boy is missing his hair. 2

"What happened to your head?" the father says, beholding his 3
skin-headed son. "Did you get a haircut?"

"I don't know," the boy replies. 4

"You don't *know* if you got a haircut? Well, tell me this: Was your head 5
with you all day?"

"I don't know," says the boy. 6

Ray Romano

My first encounter with a two-year-old came after I had gotten married 1
and become an uncle to my wife's nephew.

Until that day I wasn't really that informed about the two-year-old. Oh, I'd read 2
about them, and occasionally I'd see documentaries on the Discovery Channel showing
two-year-olds in the wild, where they belong.

But my new nephew was the first one I had seen up close. And let me tell you: If 3
you're ever out on a safari and come across one like this, stay in the Jeep.

My wife hates when I start talking about him like this. 4

"He's your nephew. You should love him." 5

I'm not saying I don't love him. I just don't want him *in* 6
my house.

Why can't I love him from afar? That's how I want to love 7
him – through pictures and folklore.

Adapted from *SeinLanguage*, *Fatherhood*, and *Everything and a Kite*

Bill
Cosby

Ray Romano

A Comprehension Check

Circle the letter of the correct answer.

1. What is Seinfeld's main point?
   a. He wishes he had his own baby.
   b. It's hard to get excited about someone else's new baby.
   c. Raising a baby is more difficult than most people think.

2. What is Cosby's main point?
   a. Children often don't communicate with their parents.
   b. Teenage boys don't like to get haircuts.
   c. The boy in the story didn't know very much.

3. What is Romano's main point?
   a. He and his wife argue about children.
   b. He doesn't love his nephew.
   c. He thinks young children are like wild animals.

B Vocabulary Study

Find the words in the comedians' anecdotes that match these definitions.

1. a strong effort to make you do something (Seinfeld) _____ (par. 1)

2. a strong feeling of interest and excitement (Seinfeld) _____ (par. 3)

3. a way of thinking (Cosby) _____ (par. 1)

4. completely (Cosby) _____ (par. 1)

5. looking at (Cosby) _____ (par. 3)

6. a meeting (Romano) _____ (par. 1)

C Paraphrasing

> **Paraphrasing means restating what you have read in your own words. By paraphrasing parts of a text, you can deepen your understanding of it.**

Choose the best paraphrase of the following sentence from the Cosby anecdote.

1. "A baseball manager has learned a lot about his job from having played the game, but a parent has not learned a thing from having once been a child."
   a. Baseball managers know a lot about their jobs because they have played baseball, but people can't learn how to be parents.
   b. Baseball managers know a lot about their jobs because they have been baseball players, but having been a child doesn't help you be a good parent.
   c. Baseball managers have played a lot of baseball, but people don't know how to be good parents just because they have been children.

Now write your own paraphrases of the following sentences on a separate piece of paper.

2. Seinfeld: "What's tough about seeing people when they have a new baby is that you have to try and match their level of enthusiasm."

3. Romano: "Until that day I wasn't really that informed about the two-year-old."

D Relating Reading to Personal Experience

Discuss these questions with your classmates.

1. Which anecdote did you think was the funniest? Why?

2. What are some good topics for telling jokes and anecdotes?

3. Do you know a good joke or anecdote? If so, tell it to your class.

> Reread one of the unit readings and time yourself. Note your reading speed in the chart on page 124.

Increasing Your Reading Speed

Good readers understand what they read, and they read at a good speed. Thus, for you to become a fluent reader in English, you need to improve your ability to understand what you are reading; you also need to improve your reading speed.

To do this, you should time yourself when you read a text that is not difficult for you. You may want to read a text several times before you time yourself, or you may want to read the text several times and time yourself after each reading. Both ways will help you improve your reading speed.

The chart on page 124 will help you keep a record of how your reading speed is improving.

After you have completed a unit, time yourself on at least one of the readings. Write down the time when you start reading the text. Then write down the time when you finish reading the text. Calculate the number of minutes and seconds it took you to read the text.

Use the chart below and on pages 122–123 to figure out your reading speed, divide the number of words in a text by the amount of time it took you to read it. That is your reading speed. For example, if the text is 425 words long and it took you five minutes and 30 seconds to read the text, your reading speed is 77.27 words per minute ($425 \div 5.5 = 77.27$).

As you go through the book, the number of words you can read in a minute should go up. That means your reading fluency is getting better.

Unit	Title of Text	Number of Words in Text	Amount of Time to Read the Text	Reading Speed (wpm=words per minute)
Unit 1 Superstitions	Two Worlds	530 words	_____ minutes & _____ seconds	_____ wpm
	Lucky Hats and Other Fishing Superstitions	517 words	_____ minutes & _____ seconds	_____ wpm
	A Superstition About New Calendars	507 words	_____ minutes & _____ seconds	_____ wpm
Unit 2 Health	Diets of the World	540 words	_____ minutes & _____ seconds	_____ wpm
	Drink, Blink, and Rest	540 words	_____ minutes & _____ seconds	_____ wpm
	Azeri Hills Hold Secret of Long Life	522 words	_____ minutes & _____ seconds	_____ wpm

Unit	Title of Text	Number of Words in Text	Amount of Time to Read the Text	Reading Speed (wpm=words per minute)
Unit 3 Remarkable Talents	The Memory Man	555 words	_____ minutes & _____ seconds	_____ wpm
	Born to Paint: Alexandra Nechita	493 words	_____ minutes & _____ seconds	_____ wpm
	Hyper-polyglots	525 words	_____ minutes & _____ seconds	_____ wpm
Unit 4 Beauty	Executives Go Under the Knife	477 words	_____ minutes & _____ seconds	_____ wpm
	What Makes a Man Attractive?	509 words	_____ minutes & _____ seconds	_____ wpm
	In the Land of the Mirror	526 words	_____ minutes & _____ seconds	_____ wpm
Unit 5 Technology	Affectionate Androids	527 words	_____ minutes & _____ seconds	_____ wpm
	Identification, Please!	462 words	_____ minutes & _____ seconds	_____ wpm
	Researchers Worry as Cyber-teens Grow Up	467 words	_____ minutes & _____ seconds	_____ wpm
Unit 6 Punishment	Spanking on Trial	512 words	_____ minutes & _____ seconds	_____ wpm
	The Letter	562 words	_____ minutes & _____ seconds	_____ wpm
	Schools Take the Fun Out of Suspension	566 words	_____ minutes & _____ seconds	_____ wpm
Unit 7 Memory	Can You Believe What You See?	490 words	_____ minutes & _____ seconds	_____ wpm
	Man Weds the Wife He Forgot	531 words	_____ minutes & _____ seconds	_____ wpm
	Repeat After Me: Memory Takes Practice	506 words	_____ minutes & _____ seconds	_____ wpm

Unit	Title of Text	Number of Words in Text	Amount of Time to Read the Text	Reading Speed (wpm=words per minute)
Unit 8 **Personality**	What Do Our Possessions Say About Us?	536 words	_____ minutes & _____ seconds	_____ wpm
	Temperament and Personality	457 words	_____ minutes & _____ seconds	_____ wpm
	Mind Your P's and Q's	540 words	_____ minutes & _____ seconds	_____ wpm
Unit 9 **Fashion**	Smart Clothes	491 words	_____ minutes & _____ seconds	_____ wpm
	Shoes	521 words	_____ minutes & _____ seconds	_____ wpm
	Style, Not Fashion	430 words	_____ minutes & _____ seconds	_____ wpm
Unit 10 **The Media**	Youth and the News Media	588 words	_____ minutes & _____ seconds	_____ wpm
	When Our Worlds Collide	501 words	_____ minutes & _____ seconds	_____ wpm
	Media Violence	536 words	_____ minutes & _____ seconds	_____ wpm
Unit 11 **Art**	Girl with a Pitcher	548 words	_____ minutes & _____ seconds	_____ wpm
	Organic Architecture	532 words	_____ minutes & _____ seconds	_____ wpm
	Could You Be a Trash Artist?	492 words	_____ minutes & _____ seconds	_____ wpm
Unit 12 **Humor**	So, Who's the Comedian?	551 words	_____ minutes & _____ seconds	_____ wpm
	Taking Humor Seriously in the Workplace	450 words	_____ minutes & _____ seconds	_____ wpm
	Three Comedians	450 words	_____ minutes & _____ seconds	_____ wpm

Reading Speed Progress Chart

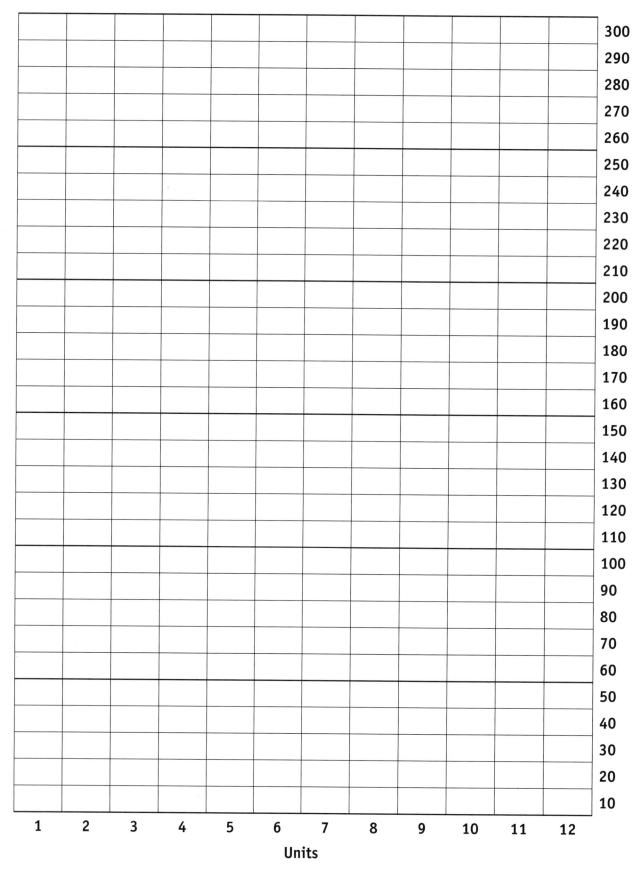

Units

Words per minute

Text and Art Credits

Text Credits

2–3   Excerpts from *Gringa Latina* by Gabriella de Ferrari. Copyright © 1995 by Gabriella de Ferrari. Reprinted by permission of Houghton Mifflin Harcourt Publishing Company & Janklow & Nesbit Associates. All rights reserved. Reprinted with permission.

5–6   Adapted from "Lucky hats and other fishing superstitions" by Tommy Braswell, *The Post and Courier*, November 25, 2001. Reprinted with permission.

8–9   Adapted from "A Superstition about New Calendars Turns Out to be a Hang-up" by Raymond Rawlinson, *The Washington Post*, December 31, 2001.

12–13   Adapted from "Diets of the World" by Sandra Gordon and Sarah Yang, *WebMD*. Reprinted with permission from Medscape.com, 2010.

15–16   Adapted from "Drink, blink and rest" by Tessa Thomas, *The European Magazine*, August 17–23, 1995. Reprinted with permission.

18–19   Adapted from "Azeri hills hold secret of long life" by Chris Morris, *Guardian Weekly*, June 29–July 5, 2000. Reprinted with permission.

22–23   Sources: http://www.guardian.co.uk/world/2009/dec/22/kim-peek-rain-man-dies; http://www.timesonline.co.uk/tol/news/world/us_and_americas/article6964730.ece; http://www.psy.dmu.ac.uk/drhiles/Savant Syndrome.htm.

25–26   Sources: "Born to Paint Alexandra Nechita may be budding Picasso," by Karen Thomas, *USA Today*, June 27, 1996, page 01D and http://www.roshe-insider.com/famous-romanians-alexandra-nechita-little-picasso.

28–29   Adapted from "Talkin' about talk" http://spinner.cofc.edu/linguist/archives/2005/11/?referrer=webcluster&. Used by permission of Michael Erard, Rick Rickerson and Equinox Publishing Ltd.

32–33   Adapted from "Executives Go Under Knife To Get Ahead" by Camillo Fracassini, *The Scotsman*, August 6, 2000. Reprinted with permission.

35–36   Adapted from "Pretty boys get the girl: What makes a man attractive?" by Brigid Schulte, *The Montreal Gazette*, Knight Ridder Newspapers, Washington, September 5, 1998. Copyright © McClatchy-Tribune Information Services. All rights reserved. Reprinted with permission.

38–39   From "In the Land of Mirror, Mirror on the Wall" by Thomas Omestad, *U.S. News & World Report*, July 23, 2001, Vol. 131, Issue 3. Copyright © 2001 U.S. News & World Report, L.P. Reprinted with permission.

42–43   Adapted from "Robots that love too much: the perils of the silicone spouse" by Graham Philips, *Sunday Age* (Melbourne, Australia), March 9, 2008. Reprinted with permission of Graham Philips.

45–46   Adapted from "Identification Please!" by Doug Smith, *Netweek*. From the website http://www.ed2go.com/news/biometrics.html.

48–49   Adapted from "Researchers Worrying as Teens Group up Online" by Patricia Wen, *The Boston Globe*, April 21, 2000. All rights reserved. Used by permission and protected by the Copyright Laws of the United States. The printing, copying, redistribution, or retransmission of the Material without express permission is prohibited.

52–53   Adapted from "Spanking on Trial: Should parents ever strike their children?" by Joe Chidley with Don Murray and Sharon Doyle Driedger, *Maclean's*, May 8, 1995.

55–56   Excerpt adapted from Chapter 15 in *Snow is Falling on Cedars*, copyright © 1994 by David Guterson. Reprinted by permission of Bloomsbury Publishing Plc and Harcourt Inc.

58–59   Adapted from "Schools are taking all the fun out of suspension" by Anna Gorman, *The Los Angeles Times*, March 13, 2000. Copyright © 2000 The Los Angeles Times. Reprinted with permission.

62–63   Adapted from "Can you believe what you see?" by Anjana Ahuja, *The Times*, September 10, 2001. Copyright © 2001 NI Syndication, London.

65–66   Adapted from "Man weds the wife he forgot – Brain cancer stole Ken's memories" by David Wilkes, *The Sunday Telegraph* (Sydney, Australia), April 29, 2001.

68–69   Adapted from "Repeat after me: Memory takes practice" by Valerie Strauss, *The Washington Post*, August 7, 2001. Copyright © The Washington Post. All rights reserved. Used by permission and protected by the Copyright Laws of the United States. The printing, copying, redistribution, or retransmission of the Material without express written permission is prohibited.

72–73   Adapted from "Booster Shots; Personal Possessions Can Be an Object Lesson" by Rosie Mestel, *The Los Angeles Times*, March 4, 2001. Copyright © 2002 The Los Angeles Times. Reprinted with permission.

75–76   Adapted from *Roots of Self* by Robert Ornstein. Published by Harper San Francisco. Copyright © 1998 by Robert Ornstein. Reprinted with permission.

78–79   Adapted from "Mind your P's and Q's," *Successful Meetings*, February 2000, Vol. 49. Copyright © 2003 VNU Business Media Inc.

82–83   Adapted from "Swedish hi-tech clothing – the perfect superhero outfit?" by Ann-Christine Andréasson. Originally produced by the University of Borås, was previously published on Sweden.se, Sweden's official website, April 24, 2009. http://www.sweden.se/eng/Home/Education/Research/Reading. Reprinted with permission.

85–86   Sources: http://hubpages.com/hub/history-of-shoes; http://www.shoeinfonet.com/about%20shoes/ history/history%20your%20shoes/history%20your%20shoes.htm; http://www.ehow.com/about_4616322_ history-of-shoes.html; http://www.runtheplanet.com/resources/historical/athleticshoes.asp.

88–89   Adapted from "The Style Imperative'" by Hara Estroff Marano, *Psychology Today*, September 1, 2008. Reprinted with permission.

92–93   Adapted from "Youth Media DNA Study of the World Association of Newspapers and News Publishers." http://www.wan-press.org/IMG/pdf/Youth_Media_DNA.pdf. Reprinted with permission.

95–96   Adapted from "When our worlds collide" by Richard Folkes, *U.S. News and World Report*, Vol. 123, September 15, 1997. Copyright © 1997 U.S. News & World Report, L.P. Reprinted with permission.

98–99   From *Viewing Violence: How Media Violence Affects Your Child's and Adolescent's Development*, by Madeline Levine. Copyright © 1996 by Madeline Levine. Used by permission of Doubleday, a division of Random House, Inc.

102–103   From *Girl with a Pearl Earring* by Tracy Chevalier. Copyright © 1999 by Tracy Chevalier. Used by permission of Plume, an imprint of Penguin Group (USA) Inc., and Gelfman Schneider Literary Agents, Inc. on behalf of the author.

105–106   Adapted from "The missing link: Architects have discovered the Holy Grail of building design – organics" by Maria Cook, *The Ottawa Citizen*, March 17, 2002. Reprinted with permission.

108–109   Adapted from "Beautiful Trash" by H. A. Schult from Deutsche Welle's English online site, DW-World.de and "Trash Art" from http://www.essortment.com/all/trash_rgnv.htm. Reprinted with permission.

112–113   Adapted from "So Who's the Comedian?; 120 Terrifying Seconds in the Spotlight at the Improv" by Gene Weingarten, *The Washington Post*, September 14, 1999. Copyright © The Washington Post. All rights reserved. Used by permission and protected by the Copyright Laws of the United States. The printing, copying, redistribution, or retransmission of the Material without express written permission is prohibited.

115–116   Adapted from "Taking Humor Seriously in the Workplace" by Steven Sultanoff. From the website www.humormatters.com/articles/workplace/htm. Reprinted with permission.

118–119   Adapted from *Sein Language* by Jerry Seinfeld, © 1993 by Jerry Seinfeld, Bantam Books. And *Everything and a Kite* by Ray Romano, © 1998 Luckykids Inc. And *Fatherhood* by Bill Cosby, © 1986 by William H Cosby, Jr., Dolphin Books (Doubleday and Company Inc).

Art Credits